HOPPÉ
PORTRAITS

HOPPÉ PORTRAITS

SOCIETY, STUDIO & STREET

Phillip Prodger and Terence Pepper

National Portrait Gallery, London

Published in Great Britain by
National Portrait Gallery Publications,
National Portrait Gallery,
St Martin's Place, London, WC2H 0HE

Published to accompany the exhibition
Hoppé Portraits: Society, Studio & Street
at the National Portrait Gallery, London
from 17 February to 30 May 2011.

This exhibition has been made possible with
the assistance of the Government Indemnity
Scheme provided by the Department for
Culture, Media and Sport and administered by
the Museums, Libraries and Archives Council.

For a complete catalogue of current
publications, please write to the National
Portrait Gallery at the address above, or visit
our website at www.npg.org.uk/publications

ISBN 978 1 85514 421 7

A catalogue record for this book is
available from the British Library.

10 9 8 7 6 5 4 3 2 1

Head of Publications: Celia Joicey
Managing Editor: Christopher Tinker
Editor: Claudia Bloch
Production Manager: Ruth Müller-Wirth
Design: Rose

Frontispiece: Margot Fonteyn, 1935

Printed in China.

Picture credits

CONTENTS

Foreword   7

E.O. Hoppé Personality and Type   10
Phillip Prodger

E.O. Hoppé A Biography   26
Terence Pepper

Fair Women   40
Studio   44
Types   116
Street   120

Chronology   166

E.O. Hoppé's Publications   170
Further Reading   171
Acknowledgements   172
Index   174

FOREWORD

E.O. Hoppé was a photographer of special talent and determination – a man whom Cecil Beaton described as 'the Master'. Although he was born in Munich, it was in Edwardian London that he developed as an outstanding practitioner of the art of photographic portraiture. He was ambitious, and within two years of establishing his own studio was exhibiting alongside great photographic artists such as Edward Steichen, Alfred Stieglitz and Alvin Langdon Coburn. His exquisite studies of the stars of drama and ballet, writers and high-society figures enabled a magazine-reading public to marvel at the beauty and poise of his subjects, as captured through the creative skill behind his lens. The studio portraits in this catalogue are accompanied by his later photojournalistic work, which shows people in the street or in daily work and his 'types', as they were referred to at the time. Projects such as *The Book of Fair Women*, published in 1922, had an unusually wide mix of portrait subjects, and clearly demonstrate that Hoppé's interests went well beyond the repressive stereotypes of the time.

A hundred years later Hoppé's portraits, although known in photographic circles, are insufficiently recognised for their outstanding artistic and technical qualities. In 1978, six years after Hoppé's death, Terence Pepper, Curator of Photographs, organised the exhibition *Camera Portraits by E.O. Hoppé* at the National Portrait Gallery. It is a particular pleasure for the Gallery to return to this brilliant artist and present a new selection of Hoppé's work in collaboration with the E.O. Hoppé Estate Collection at Curatorial Assistance, Pasadena.

I am very grateful to Graham Howe, of Curatorial Assistance, who first proposed that this would be the time to reconsider Hoppé's portraits, and has been an excellent collaborator in all aspects of the project. My considerable thanks also go to Phillip Prodger, Curator of Photography at the Peabody Essex Museum, who has curated the exhibition, and to Terence Pepper, who has advised throughout and has updated his biographical essay on Hoppé for this catalogue.

I am also very grateful to Sophie Clark, Exhibitions Manager and Claudia Bloch, Editor, who have worked with the support of Sarah Tinsley, Celia Joicey and Christopher Tinker. There are many others at the Gallery I should also thank, including Pim Baxter, Andrea Easey, Denise Ellitson, Flora Fricker, Justine McLisky, Eleanor Macnair, Ruth Müller-Wirth, Doris Pearce, Jude Simmons, Ulrike Wachsmann and Helen Whiteoak.

Sandy Nairne
Director, National Portrait Gallery

ESSAYS

—

E.O. HOPPÉ
PERSONALITY AND TYPE
Phillip Prodger

Standing on a Paris rooftop in the chill of night, Emil Otto Hoppé, one of the pre-eminent photographers of his generation, peered into the darkness and weighed up the challenge before him. It was 1911, and he had come expecting to photograph the formidable French statesman Georges Clemenceau, the former Communard so ruthless he was nicknamed 'le Tigre'. In the decade that was to follow, Clemenceau, during his second term as Prime Minister, would lead his country through the First World War and help broker the Treaty of Versailles. But at the hour appointed for his sitting with Hoppé, he was still in the bath. After a long wait, repeated apologies from his servant and muffled grumblings behind closed doors, the politician finally emerged on the roof, bearing little resemblance to his larger-than-life reputation. The stooped figure, a 'shivering little man in a nightshirt' Hoppé later wrote, gazed apprehensively into the camera.[1] 'No man is a hero to his valet,' he reflected, recalling the words of Madame Cornuel, 'let alone his photographer.'[2] But Hoppé had travelled across Europe for this opportunity, and there was little time to waste. So he found Clemenceau a new set of clothes and proceeded to make the picture, chatting about things the statesman knew well – his writings, for example, or a forthcoming vote in parliament. Hoppé always prepared for such visits by reading as much as he could about his sitters and their interests. By degrees, Clemenceau let down his guard. When at last he seemed natural, Hoppé fired the shutter. The story of the unlikely sitting was to be saved for reminiscences and memoirs. The picture would show only the person the public admired (right).[3]

Georges Clemenceau, 1911

Hoppé made a name for himself as one of the leading portraitists of his generation. And like most successful photographers, he was careful to cultivate the right clientele. Charming, handsome and well-connected, he was completely at ease in celebrity circles, but he would not have risen to the position he had were it not for his tremendous talent and extraordinary ability to capture the psychology of his subjects. Hoppé was seldom content merely to depict a person against a pleasing backdrop; he strived to provide insight, and to help the viewer grasp something elusive about a sitter. His photographs do not just document what celebrities looked like, they reveal the kind of people they were. Whether strong or vulnerable, shy or brash, Hoppé attempted to convey the essence of the person depicted. As he got to know his sitters better, he came to understand them. Through his pictures he attempted to share this understanding.

Had he simply been the most accomplished portrait photographer of his day, Hoppé would have deserved his place in history, but he also had a restless mind, and was intent on making sense of what he saw and photographed. From his unique perspective as photographer to the stars, he began to wonder what it was that made certain people succeed where others failed. His extraordinary access to leaders in various professions prompted him to consider whether they might share common characteristics. What, for example, makes a dancer a dancer, or a writer a writer? Hoppé was not just interested in meeting famous and glamorous people. He wanted to know what made them succeed, what shaped their personalities, and how they arrived at the circumstances of their lives.

Hoppé visited this question of 'types' repeatedly throughout the 1920s and 1930s. As he struggled to understand the relationship between the jobs people did and the people they were, his fascination with the correlation between personality and type became one of the hallmarks of his career. Living and working in early twentieth-century London, Hoppé witnessed unprecedented social mobility and cultural and racial integration. He wished to record the transformations he saw around him, and examine questions of wealth and social standing. His goal was to create a collective portrait made up of various photographs of people from all walks of life.

Hoppé saw celebrities as few others did. He knew what matinée idols looked like without makeup, and the appearance of politicians in their dressing gowns. Customers visit a portrait studio much as patients might go to a doctor's surgery, their bodily secrets held in strict confidence. Like a physician, a photographer comes to know their imperfections, blemishes and boils, wigs and girdles. If the world sees a sitter's 'right' side, the photographer knows the other one – in which the hair doesn't sit quite right, the face looks gaunt or chubby, wizened or immature. Hoppé was generous about such things. 'The personality of living people,' he wrote, 'dual and often multifold, is always more absorbing than that portrayed on canvas, and I have been lucky in that my calling as a portraitist has enabled me to peek behind the façades, as it were, of so many great and interesting men and women.'[4]

Hoppé found that people were often more interesting than they first appeared. Clemenceau, for example, proved to be much more engaging than he seemed. 'His valet worshipped him,' he recalled, 'and before long I was equally impressed.'[5] His features were those of a shopkeeper, but 'his hands provided an instant key to his character,' Hoppé wrote. 'Strong, ruthless, daring. Hands such as those would never have been content to rest on a counter.'[6] It was a lesson Hoppé would recount in his 1945 autobiography *Hundred Thousand Exposures*, and one he applied to his own work throughout his career. Facial expressions can be controlled, he explained, but hands are often overlooked.[7]

Although his portraits were frequently reduced to headshots for publication, Hoppé usually took pictures full bust or full figure in the negative, wide enough to capture the hands and torso. This fascination with hands is one of the qualities that often distinguishes a Hoppé portrait, in his photograph of the dancer Margot Fonteyn (p.56), for example, or Gina Palerme in top hat and tails (p.67), Sir Arthur Conan Doyle at his desk (p.94), or Edward Gordon Craig with his hands in his pockets (p.62). Hands can be assertive, deferential, weathered or silken. They can be held with confidence or helplessness. In Hoppé's view, they were a window on character. In his self-portrait of 1910 (p.8), the photographer stares directly at the camera with piercing eyes, two fingers pressed into his cheek. His left hand cradles his chin, the angled cuff of his jacket glancing off the edge of the frame. The portrait reveals the considerable control Hoppé exerted over his compositions. The depth of field is narrow, so that focus is centred on the plane of the photographer's eyes, allowing his ears and nose to fall into blurry abstraction. Only his eyes, hands and forehead are sharp. It is a portrait befitting the cocky young photographer: his eyes, omniscient like a lens; his hand, sure, reflecting the dexterity of his craft; the imposing cranium housing the creative mind.

Using shallow focus to emphasise certain features and suppress others was a technique Hoppé would have known from the work of the Victorian photographer Julia Margaret Cameron, whom he admired; not only did Hoppé describe her as one of the 'great photographers of the past' in his autobiography, he also claimed a personal connection with her, as he believed she had occasionally photographed in his studios at Millais House when it belonged to prior occupant John Everett Millais.[8] Although this claim is unsubstantiated, Hoppé was mindful of the association, and the deep chiaroscuro evident in his self-portrait was a favourite Cameron motif.[9] His face materialises out of inky darkness, the background indistinct. Hoppé presents himself with confidence and intensity, yet he addresses his attention to the viewer. He made a career out of closely hewn observation.

The Studio and Beyond

Hoppé was an artist of extraordinary range, who was just as comfortable photographing on the street as he was in the studio. Throughout his career he alternated between photographing the most famous people of the time and others whom few recognised. When the allure of high society deserted him, he camped with Romanian gypsies for months on end, or sailed to Australia to record aboriginal settlements. He was a social chameleon, as comfortable in London's Limehouse or New York's Bowery as he was in the drawing rooms of Europe. It was this, perhaps more than any other quality, that made him such a unique figure. Arguably, no other photographer in history enjoyed such fluid mobility between society's upper echelons and its lowest rungs.

And so it was that at age eighty-seven or so, the indefatigable Hoppé sat down to write a second autobiography. *Hundred Thousand Exposures* had appeared some twenty years earlier, and there was more to recount. With shaky pen, the elderly artist recorded his thoughts on a leaf of notepaper. 'Russian Ballet – Karsavina, Nijinsky, Pavlova ... Diaghilev. Reinhardt's production of the *Miracle* ..., and Reinhardt's staging of Molière's comedy *Le malade imaginaire* in the rooms of his castle at Leopoldskron before an invited audience.' A few more names followed, but the list tapered off. He considered the false start,

An example of E.O. Hoppé's textile designs

put the pen down, and set the page aside. Some time later – hours, or maybe weeks – he picked it up again. This time his pen was more confident, the hand quicker. 'Among the outstanding events in the course of my professional career,' he proclaimed, 'I might mention my connection with the Russian Ballet, Reinhardt's, George Bernard Shaw, my recollections as a beauty judge, and many others.' He annotated the passage 'Start Here,' underlined it, marked it with an asterisk and drew an arrow.

While Hoppé would never finish the manuscript for his second autobiography, this book and the exhibition it accompanies address each of the themes highlighted in Hoppé's notes. The Ballets Russes, with its synaesthesia of dance, music, set and stage design, held a special place for Hoppé. An artistic polymath, he dabbled in set and costume design himself, and produced sumptuous designs for textiles inspired by the ballet (opposite). The theatre impresario Max Reinhardt taught Hoppé the importance of drama in portraiture; his photographs of actors and film stars bore this influence directly. Hoppé's interest in typology, class and social structure was exemplified by the works of the playwright and social agitator George Bernard Shaw. And Hoppé's experience as a beauty judge, precipitated by the publication of his encyclopaedic *Book of Fair Women* in 1922, reflected a lifetime spent analysing human aesthetics.

Hoppé lived the sort of life of which others might only dream. He travelled widely, and always went first class. In India he dined with maharajas, and in Hollywood he sipped cocktails with the stars. He was called to Buckingham Palace to photograph the King. Writers, philosophers and scientists visited his studio, while magazines and journals commissioned him to photograph persons of note. His clients included prime ministers and presidents, aristocrats and tribal chiefs, dictators and revolutionaries. To be photographed by Hoppé spoke of achievement. Those wanting to make it big hoped a sitting would bring them fame, others sought proof they had arrived. Avant-garde artists had him take their pictures and invited him to their soirées. The influence of his sitters was inestimable: separately they shaped the Harlem Renaissance, the Bauhaus, the Bloomsbury Group, Vorticism and the Ballets Russes. His associates in photographic circles shaped the course of photographic history.

The late photohistorian Bill Jay described Hoppé as the most famous photographer in the world in the 1920s. 'To say that someone has become a "household name",' he wrote, 'has become a cliché, yet in Hoppé's case the phrase is apt. Rarely in the history of the medium has a photographer been so famous in his own lifetime among the general public.'[10] In the preface to *Hundred Thousand Exposures*, the illustrious photographer Cecil Beaton agreed, describing Hoppé succinctly as 'the Master'.[11] It was an acknowledgement of Hoppé's pre-eminence, but it was also written in tribute, with the realisation that the older photographer was unlikely to enjoy the success he once did.

Although Hoppé continued to photograph after the Second World War, he was by that time in his late sixties, and had given up the daily grind of maintaining a busy studio. His energies mainly went into managing his Dorien Leigh picture library, comprised of his personal inventory of photographs and pictures bought from other sources, which he licensed to magazines and other commercial interests. Hoppé used the name Dorien Leigh as a pseudonym on his own photographs at various times throughout his career, but inconsistently. For this reason it can be difficult to attribute Hoppé photographs based on the Dorien Leigh studio stamp alone. Fortunately, the E.O. Hoppé Estate Collection at Curatorial Assistance, Pasadena, retains the artist's daybooks, so it is usually possible to ascertain not only the maker of a photograph but often the precise day on which a particular photograph was made.

Through Dorien Leigh, Hoppé's photographs continued to be seen and distributed. And although Hoppé added photographs in the years that followed, his reputation rested primarily on the three decades between the opening of his first studio in Baron's Court in 1907 and the outbreak of war in 1939. 'Hoppé's pictures were entirely different from other photographs of that period,' Beaton explained, 'for they were all imbued with a controlled and subtle romanticism and atmospheric glow – they were the work of someone with taste, perception, appreciation; of someone who used the camera as an artist.'[12]

Hoppé straddled two distinct periods in photographic history. When he began his career, Pictorialism dominated photographic salons. Using coloured and textured papers, hand-made emulsions, and soft-focus lenses, Pictorialists sought to make photographs that resembled drawings or prints. Their aim was to win photography elevated status by demonstrating that it is a plastic medium, capable of producing pictures as expressive as traditional media. Early Hoppé portraits, such as those he made of the artists William Nicholson (p.80) and William Strang (p.87), the actress Teddie Gerrard (p.74) and the dancer Clotilde von Derp (p.55) reflect this sensibility – dreamy, languid and romantic. In the 1920s Hoppé largely jettisoned this style in favour of a harder-edged Modernism; figures were shown directly and with minimal artifice. Hoppé's photographs of Benito Mussolini (p.111) and the dancers Ted Shawn (p.44) and Tilly Losch (p.59) exemplify this mode – bold, impassive and uncompromising.

When it came to equipment, Hoppé had a utilitarian approach. He shot mainly in black and white, but experimented with hand-coloured gravures and new colour-printing techniques. His exquisite Carbro Colour prints of the models Biddy Willoughby and Eileen Hawthorne (pp.76–7) demonstrate remarkable facility with the complex medium. The photographer was required to make separate negatives selecting for red, green and blue, which were then recombined in the print by superimposing corresponding layers of pigmented carbon tissue in perfect registration. While most of his studio photographs were made with bellows-type view cameras, ranging in format from English quarter-plate (4¼ x 3¼ inches) to 10 x 8 inches in glass, nitrate and safety film, he also used twin-lens reflex cameras in different medium-format (120 film) sizes. Moreover, Hoppé appears to have been one of the first professional photographers to use the Leica I camera, as many of his street photographs of London and Germany in the mid-1920s were taken on newly introduced 35mm film. Hoppé believed in using whatever technology was necessary to get the best results. Such practicality was fundamental to the success of the Dorien Leigh picture library, which depended on having a wide assortment of images taken in various situations.

Ironically, Dorien Leigh may have contributed to the decline of Hoppé's reputation in the latter half of the twentieth century. Like most picture libraries, it was organised according to subject, not by artist. As the library grew, Hoppé's images were subsumed within it, becoming increasingly difficult to appreciate as a distinct group. Later, when Dorien Leigh's holdings were sold to the vast Mansell Collection, Hoppé's photographs were overwhelmed by other holdings. Although they remained individually accessible, finding them was difficult, and the cohesion of Hoppé's life's work was hard to ascertain. In 1994, when the Hoppé archive was extracted from the Mansell Collection by curator Graham Howe, ten years of conservation and cataloguing began and the pieces were reassembled to form an archive of his works. Most of the photographs that appear in this volume are drawn from this reconstituted E.O. Hoppé Estate Collection, the largest repository of the photographer's work. Hoppé lived to the age of ninety-four, and the collection reflects the remarkable diversity of his output.

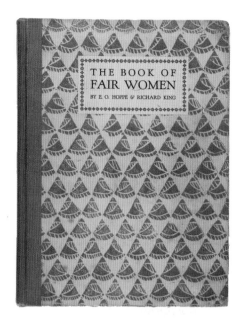

The Book of Fair Women, published 1922
London Types, published 1926

Hoppé's photographs of celebrities in the 1910s, 1920s and 1930s are well known. Less familiar are the street pictures he made in the same period, which are brimming with humour, affection and insight. Although he was born and brought up in continental Europe, as an adult Hoppé made London his home. Collectively, his photographs of the peoples of England are a love letter to his adopted country. They playfully indulge the stereotypes of English life – butlers and bobbies, sipping tea and having a pint at the local pub. Yet they have a serious side too. Hoppé was among the first photographers to investigate the diversity of peoples who made the capital their home in the early twentieth century. His photographs provide a rare glimpse of the East and South Asian, North African and Caribbean communities that made London an international centre. He photographed these various groups with dedicated interest.

In a short article entitled 'A Study of Ethnography on London's Pavements', Hoppé even proposed that London might serve as an excellent laboratory for an aspiring anthropologist. 'Passers-by from many nations in Europe or, for that matter, from the Middle and Far East, the Dominions and the USA are encountered on the pavements of our large towns,' he noted. 'They are accepted as part of the community in general.'[13] He continued: 'the new chapter of ethnology sets out to show how the race retains its own characteristics, despite any uniforming process of civilisation or standardisation, in classes where it has been said there are no national borders. Despite any attributions of cosmopolitan life, the race element resists uniform environment, uniform luxuries. The pearls, the furs, the habits of the leisured world, have no power to compete with racial contours.'[14] The camera, Hoppé believed, could be instrumental in examining this new social dynamic.

Hoppé's shuttling between studio and street was driven by two distinct projects, which rank among his most significant achievements: *The Book of Fair Women* and *London Types*. In 1922 *The Book of Fair Women* was published, a compilation of thirty-two portraits of women whom Hoppé had photographed, and whom he considered the most beautiful he had ever seen (opposite, top). Considering the circles in which he travelled and the number of sitters who visited him, the book represented a remarkable cross-section of society, and the inclusion, or exclusion, of particular sitters created something of a sensation. The idea of collecting images of archetypal female beauty was itself an engaging one, but Hoppé flouted convention by making his selection both international and multi-racial, so that the women who appeared in the book should represent the pinnacle of attractiveness around the world. The selections stirred controversy, while at the same time securing his reputation as a connoisseur of the female form. The publication of the book raised real philosophical questions about human aesthetics. But it was also good for business, as women clamoured to be anointed the next great Hoppéan beauty, sometimes at the insistence of their husbands.[15]

Hoppé's interest in beauty paralleled an abiding concern with social types, which culminated in the publication of his book *London Types* in 1926 (opposite, bottom). *London Types* followed the related book *Taken from Life*, published in 1922. In each case a suite of photographs was accompanied by semi-fictional accounts of the sitters' lives, each intended to provide insight into social problems of the working class. The advertisement for *Taken from Life* described it as 'seven studies of humanity taken from life. All but one of these are taken from the lower strata of society, although some of them have achieved a relative success in their own world … The seven characters so admirably described and photographed can never be forgotten by the reader. The seven studies are: a Tramp; a Cabman; a Drug-fiend; a Pedlar; an old Countrywoman; a Courtesan, and a Charwoman.'[16]

The two poles of his practice could hardly have been more extreme. On one hand, he served the most exclusive patrons in Europe and enjoyed widespread recognition as an authority on feminine beauty. On the other, he was to be found photographing social cast-offs; drug addicts, prostitutes and the mentally ill. Whatever fault one might find with the science behind Hoppé's examinations of beauty and type, one can only admire his attempts to use his unique position to analyse social injustice. By combining personal observations of sitters and their behaviours with visual evidence, he tried to understand the sociological forces that govern human interaction.

Typology and the Street

Hoppé's ventures in street photography undoubtedly helped to refine his talents in the studio and refreshed his interest in formal portraiture. As exciting as it could be to meet celebrities, many were difficult and monotony could set in after weeks spent under the studio lamps at Millais House. Moreover, the business of portrait photography was itself in transition. 'When I began professional photography, sitters visited the studio as a matter of course,' Hoppé remarked in his autobiography.[17] 'But the advent of miniature cameras caused the most profound and significant changes in technique. The speed of modern films and the power of the lenses, the advent of portable lighting units which can be packed in a suitcase, make it possible for the photographer to visit clients in their own homes.'[18] Being able to visit a sitter in his or her home enabled the photographer to obtain portraits of those who were reluctant to visit the studio, such as the notoriously shy author Thomas Hardy (p.93). At the same time, it made it possible to provide viewers with a glimpse of a sitter's private life, as in Hoppé's innovative portrait of King George V at his writing desk (p.107); or to place the sitter in a significant site, as with his portrait of Jacob Epstein posing in front of his magnificent memorial for Oscar Wilde (p.81).

Liberated from the studio, Hoppé was free to pursue his instincts wherever they led. Naturally, he remained mindful of the marketability of the

Frederick Foxcroft by
Sir Benjamin Stone, 1897

Farm Labourers by
Sir Benjamin Stone, 1890s

subjects he photographed, and not every project was of his choosing, as he was frequently given assignments by illustrated weekly magazines. Nevertheless, there is a remarkable consistency to his approach that transcends the specific requirements of the jobs he accepted. On the street, he gravitated towards moments of irony and quirkiness. He frequently photographed people living outside the mainstream, and 'down and outs': pieceworkers, the unemployed and people sleeping rough. Such pictures were not without political charge, and Hoppé's enduring affection for George Bernard Shaw might fairly be seen as sympathy for the playwright's strident socialist views. Verbally, as a society photographer, it was necessary for him to keep his political opinions close to his chest. In pictures, however, he had license to explore the issues that mattered to him.

In 1909, just two years into his practice, Hoppé was one of two photographers chosen to oversee the British pavilions at the giant International Photographic Exhibition in Dresden. His co-organiser, Sir Benjamin Stone, became a close friend and remained an influence throughout his career. In 1897 Stone had founded an organisation called the National Photographic Record Association (NPRA), which flourished until around 1910. The purpose of the NPRA was to document the customs and festivals of England, such as local pageants, dances, ceremonies and occupations, which were in danger of vanishing in an increasingly modern and multi-cultural country (opposite, bottom). Although they followed a well-established pattern of nineteenth-century practice, with precedent in John Thomson's series *Street Life in London* (1878–9) and Peter Henry Emerson's book *Life and Landscape on the Norfolk Broads* (1886), Stone's photographs had a unique inflection. Stone photographed the English much as nineteenth-century anthropologists photographed in Africa, Oceania or Asia – with curiosity, surprise and a hint of detachment. It was as if the camera, which British explorers had focused on other cultures, had finally been aimed at Britons themselves. In Stone's photographs the English appear quaint, tribal and mired in historical traditions.

Hoppé's later investigations of English social types shared Stone's democratic approach. Whereas Hoppé's intention was to record modern English characteristics, Stone hoped through his efforts to distinguish between traditional behaviours of the English race. Two years after his election to Parliament, in 1897, Stone famously photographed everyone passing through Speaker's Gate at the Palace of Westminster. In all he produced more than 1,200 photographs of people from all walks of life participating in the life of the institution, from ministers to members of the public, plumbers, cleaners and, in the case of Frederick Foxcroft, the foreman painter (opposite, top).

Stone was not the only photographer to examine social hierarchies in the early twentieth century, and indeed, the depiction of ideal types has a long history in art.[19] In Hoppé's own time August Sander began photographing representative German types in the 1910s. Photographs such as *Mother and Daughter* of 1912 reflect his determination to produce archetypal images of peoples of different ages, sexes and occupations (right). Although Sander conceived of the atlas *People of the Twentieth Century* (*Menschen des 20. Jahrhunderts*) in the mid-1920s, it was not until 1929 that a selection of sixty portraits from the series was published in *The Face of Our Time* (*Antlitz der Zeit*).[20] Hoppé's *London Types* had been published three years earlier, in 1926.

The reasons Hoppé gave for photographing types paralleled those that motivated both Stone and Sander. Some years later Hoppé explained, 'I had it in my mind to make a record of the various distinctive types which one used to see in the London streets but which were rapidly vanishing as the result of changing conditions. I started on this pictorial chronicle by approaching any

Mother and Daughter: Farmer's Wife and Miner's Wife by August Sander, 1912

interesting "characters" wherever I chanced to come across them, telling them quite frankly of my intentions and asking them to come to my studio to be photographed. On the whole, and much to my surprise, I met with fewer refusals than I had expected, although I occasionally found myself involved in embarrassing situations.'[21] He did not elaborate on what those situations were, but he was at pains to explain that he behaved ethically in obtaining his typological photographs.

During the 1920s unscrupulous photographers built extensive picture libraries by inviting sitters to 'free' sittings; the victim traded rights to his or her image for a copy of their portrait. Hoppé bristled: 'This pernicious racket, which in other walks of life would be rightly condemned as unprofessional conduct, was originated by firms of West End photographers which developed the idea of making "collections" of people belonging to various professions and social groups. Authors, clergy, society leaders and doctors were among those subtly flattered by an invitation to a "free sitting." It was a cheap and undignified way of obtaining something for nothing and few, if any, realised that they had no control over these portraits since the copyright was vested in the photographer who could use them for any purpose.'[22] Hoppé was being discreet in withholding the names of those wronged. Elsewhere in his notes he recorded that his friend George Bernard Shaw was among those conned by the promise of a free sitting.[23] Photographing types not only held the promise of advancing human knowledge, they were potentially lucrative as well.

In his photographs of London types, Hoppé followed the conventions established in his studio. Sitters were photographed against neutral backgrounds in deep chiaroscuro, their faces evenly illuminated with a slight emphasis from above. This gentle top lighting had an ennobling effect on the sitters, who were shown either head-on or in partial profile. In contrast to his studio portraits, however, he did not usually photograph 'types' full figure. Instead, they are shown either head-only or as busts. Tighter cropping eliminated the details of the sitters that gave them their individuality, and helped them seem more generalised. Unlike conventional studio portraits that celebrate the personality of the subject, in Hoppé's types character is subsumed to role.

To Hoppé, questions of beauty and occupation were inextricably linked. Arguing that individuals manifest their character in their faces, he maintained that hard-working people develop particular attractiveness. 'Beauty knows no class distinctions,' he wrote.[24] 'Flower girls and charladies, nowadays designated pompously as "cleaners", are certainly to be numbered amongst my most beautiful sitters,' he explained.[25] 'A philosophy garnered from a life of toil, a brave resignation to circumstance, and, last but not least, that matchless sense of humour which is a substitute for contentment, stamps their faces with a spiritual beauty which may not be bought in any beauty parlour.'[26] Accordingly, his photographs of a flower seller, charwomen and others served a dual purpose (pp.117–19). They were physiognomic studies of particular occupational types, but they were also an extension of his investigations of beauty. Although photographs of these women did not make it into the pages of *The Book of Fair Women,* he nevertheless viewed them as related.

Strangely, the verbal descriptions of Hoppé's types were liable to change according to circumstance, as the artist would label and relabel typological portraits according to need. Thus, a *Kentish Type* might be reclassified as a *Polish Peasant*, a *Jewish Type* would later be called *A Scholar*; *Mothers* could also be found as *Home Workers* (p.117); and, most peculiarly, the elderly man described as *Prime of Life* performed double duty as a *Bavarian Small Holder* and a *Dutch Farmer* (p.117). In an article for the *Sunday*

Charlady, 1920s, from *London Types*

Express, several of the types appearing in this volume were co-opted for the story 'Fashions in Beards from Many Lands'. Consequently, the *London Type* published in *London Types* as *Highly Respectable* (p.119), became *An Old English Sailor*, a *New York Type* became *A Moscow Style*, and the *Jewish Type* and *Scholar* described above morphed into *A French Astronomer*.[27] Some of this prevarication may be ascribed to faulty memory, or the caprice of national borders – in New York, for example, Hoppé found Haitian types and German types, although each could also properly be identified as American. The motivation, however, was probably also financial, as the more often one could license a particular photograph, the more profitable it would become – when a particular photograph could serve plausibly to depict a type not otherwise represented in the library, it was conveniently reclassified. This is a problem that is repeated in the portraits included in *The Book of Fair Women,* in which nationalities were equally plastic.

In accordance with other popular books of the day, Hoppé's 'types' were occasionally given a moral dimension. Hoppé befriended the illustrator and caricaturist George Belcher with whom he exchanged pictures. It was an arrangement that suited both. 'I would send along to him choice specimens of the dying-out races of muffin-men and venerable "cabbies" he would pass on to me some of his cheerful and quick-witted flower girls and genteel charwomen,' Hoppé recalled.[28] Belcher was expert in drawing London characters, contributing his studies to a variety of publications, most notably *Odd Fish: Being a Casual Selection of London Residents Described and Drawn* (1923) by Stacy Aumonier.[29] For *Taken from Life* and *London Types,* Hoppé commissioned writers to produce fictional biographies based on his photographs. The science-fiction author J.D. Beresford produced the text for *Taken from Life*, while the humorist William Pett Ridge wrote for *London Types.* The woman Hoppé identified as a *Charlady* was reproduced in *Taken from Life* in an alternate pose biting an apple, symbolising her sexual transgressions and identified as 'Sophy' (opposite). Beresford wrote, 'There is a class among the very poor, as there is also a class among the very rich, that has little regard for sexual morality ... I do not wish to imply that this sexual morality is solely a consequence of an economic condition, but I maintain that there is a recognisable relation between them. And in dealing with the very poor we have to face the unpleasant truth that marriage is commonly fatal to happiness.'[30] Monogamy, Beresford went on to explain, was impossible for the woman. 'As a girl, Sophy no doubt set her teeth bravely into the apple of life and bit hard.'[31]

Lessons from Shaw
As author or co-author of twenty-seven books, Hoppé had occasion to collaborate with numerous writers, and as a portraitist he photographed many of the leading literary figures of the period. But it was George Bernard Shaw whom he singled out for special praise. The anecdote may be apocryphal, but Hoppé claimed that the two were introduced when Shaw, impressed by an exhibition of Hoppé's works at the Goupil Gallery, Regent Street, in 1922, wrote to the photographer with the brief cryptic invitation, 'they say I photograph well'.[32] Hoppé responded with an invitation that Shaw sit for a portrait at Millais House, which, according to the story, he eagerly accepted. This aspect of the account seems unlikely, as most known portraits Hoppé took of Shaw appear to have been made in the writer's home at 10 Adelphi Terrace in central London (pp.114–15), and no studio portraits are preserved either in the E.O. Hoppé Estate Collection or the Shaw Papers in the manuscripts collection of the London School of Economics, the main repository of relevant pictures and documents.

George Bernard Shaw
and pavement artist, 1924

Shaw, who was a prolific amateur photographer, accompanied Hoppé more than once on his street photography expeditions. On one such occasion, Shaw appears as an observer in a photograph of a pavement artist that Hoppé revealed was set up (above). 'I knew a young portrait painter whose efforts to make his work known had failed him and who was forced to earn a bare living as a pavement artist, with a pitch on the Embankment. Shaw lived at the time at No.9 Whitehall Court, which is just around the corner. I told him of my young friend and suggested that he should look at the pastel drawings and allow me to photograph him doing so. Shaw readily agreed and the resulting publicity helped a great deal to establish the artist's reputation.'[33]

Hoppé and Shaw's common interest in photography prompted a variety of discussions, ranging from the appropriate use of coloured filters in black-and-white photography to whether the medium could rightly claim to be a fine art. The two concluded that though it is 'primarily a recording medium … [it] can become a vehicle for the expression of emotional and artistic values, provided the tools of the craft are used with due regard to the limitations imposed by the medium.'[34] On one occasion Hoppé showed Shaw a collection of photographs he had made of clouds. Shaw responded that photographs of weather were of great interest to him, so the two travelled to Putney Common together to photograph cloud formations.[35] The photographs of clouds preserved in the Shaw Papers may have resulted from one or more of these joint outings (opposite).

If Hoppé and Shaw's friendship inspired Shaw to improve his photography, it also prompted Hoppé to think more deeply about typology and character. Shaw, after all, built his reputation on plays such as *Pygmalion* (1912), a satire of class distinctions that faced head on the question of nature versus nurture in relation to social success. In his voluminous notes on Shaw, Hoppé referred repeatedly to this aspect of their association. 'Crusade against snobbishness, petty conventionalities, false generalities, attacking social evils and respectable shibboleths,' Hoppé noted.[36] In Shaw, he had found a kindred spirit, resistant to the notion that class is predestined, and determined to discover what was genuine in people, regardless of wealth or status.

Cloud study by George Bernard Shaw, *c.*1933

Although energised by such talk, Hoppé did not stop photographing the celebrities on whom his livelihood depended; indeed, in spite of his democratic rhetoric he continued to profess excitement when glamorous sitters visited the studio. Nor was Millais House a socialistic place. Visitors remained impressed with the Epstein bust of Iris Tree that stylishly adorned his grand piano and the Puvis de Chavannes aquatints that hung in his library.[37]

Nevertheless, encouraged by his interactions with Shaw and others, Hoppé rededicated himself to street photography, producing some of the most remarkable photographs of the period. He had learned how to take full advantage of his position, nurturing his reputation as a pre-eminent celebrity portraitist while simultaneously probing new directions in picture-making.

On assignment for the *Graphic,* he was asked to photograph in London's East End. The Chinese community at Limehouse was known to be particularly inhospitable. 'A charming people, but intruders were, to put it mildly, non personae gratae,' he confided.[38] Undeterred, Hoppé befriended a shopkeeper named Wu Kang. Wu's daughter had accepted a post in Liverpool, and Hoppé provided photographs of the two so they could remember each other while they were separated. Grateful for his kindness, Wu provided introductions enabling him to enter local Chinese clubs. There he perfected a method of undercover photographing. He bought the quietest camera he could find, a cheap fixed-focus Brownie, and wrapped it in brown paper, tearing a small hole in the makeshift parcel so the lens could see out. He placed the parcel on a table of the right height, lit his pipe as a diversion, and released the shutter. Exposure was tricky to calculate and winding on to the next frame required mysterious juggling with the parcel. Nevertheless, the subterfuge produced several photographs suitable for publication.[39] Unfortunately, when news of the photographs spread, Hoppé was no longer able to visit Limehouse interiors comfortably. But he continued to use the method in other venues. The candid photographs he took of men drinking in pubs, playing cards in Islamic cafés and eating in refreshment rooms (p.135), for example, were almost certainly made with this technique. Hoppé's surreptitious photographs of restaurant interiors made him one of an august group of pioneers. Paul Strand photographed with a false lens as early as the mid-1910s, whereas Walker Evans did not begin photographing using a hidden camera on the New York subway until 1938.

A French-educated, Austro-German émigré Hoppé may have been, but he fully absorbed the British taste for the absurd. His photographs of a girl grieving in a pet cemetery (p.156), a woman embracing an organ pipe suggestively at Royal Albert Hall, (p.159), or gap-toothed young men chatting over soup and milkshakes at a London snack bar (pp.136–7), for example, are tongue-in-cheek but heartfelt considerations of the British psyche. This approach prefigured the satirical photographer Tony Ray-Jones (p.22), whose attempts to survey British character by photographing people at leisure in the late 1960s influenced contemporary photographers such as Martin Parr.[40] Similar to Hoppé's motivation for photographing people in their day-to-day lives, Ray-Jones's aim was to 'communicate something of the spirit and the mentality of the English, their habits and way of life, the ironies that exist in the way they do things, partly through tradition and partly through the nature of their environment.'[41]

Glyndebourne by
Tony Ray-Jones, 1967

Hoppé's experiences photographing on the street reinforced his views
on beauty and type. 'You examine the English types,' he surmised, 'compare them,
extract the common denominators, and formulate certain rules, only to find that
the beauties of Japan, China, India, Hawaii and Russia are the negation of all the
qualities that constitute the beauty of the Englishwoman. And yet who would deny
that they possess beauty of a different kind?'[42] From national character to racial
aesthetics, Hoppé worked to understand how individual portraits might serve as
archetypes, standing in for classes of individuals. The next step was to compare
these archetypes to each other. In a brief paper titled 'Rhythm of Perfect Types'
he attempted to construct a unifying theory to reconcile his abiding interests in
typology and achievement. The beauty of the women he photographed, or their
lack of it, became the centrepiece of his investigation.

Beauty – The Ultimate Type

Hoppé's interest in feminine beauty poured fuel on the fire of his career,
solidifying his reputation as a portrait photographer without equal. Given his
unique position as photographer to the greatest celebrities of his age and his
international outlook, he was perfectly situated to produce a study of beautiful
women from around the world. *The Book of Fair Women*, published by Jonathan
Cape in London, F. Bruckmann in Germany and Alfred Knopf in New York, was
illustrated with exquisite photogravures and covered in handmade paper
designed by the photographer. The effects of these books on public opinion
far exceeded the number of copies sold, and Hoppé would spend the rest of
his life fielding questions about beauty, writing thought-papers and serving
as an arbiter of good taste.

Most of the women included in the book were British and American,
reflecting the sitters who patronised his studio, and not all were famous. He
made it a point not to confine his choices to obvious candidates. The book was
distinguished from similar contemporary collections by the inclusion of women
of other nationalities – not just 'exotic' (to British eyes) European women from
Italy, Spain, Greece and Poland, but women of noticeably different skin colour
from places as far flung as China, Japan, India, Africa, the Caribbean and the

'Dorothy Darnit' comic strip, 1922

South Pacific. Hoppé argued that women of other cultures were at least as beautiful as Europeans, although he conceded one might have to belong to the culture concerned to fully appreciate it (pp.41–3).

This slight caveat aside, the idea that beauty could be found in any race was provocative. The *Scarborough Post* was scandalised. '"The Book of Fair Women," which Mr. E.O. Hoppé has just produced, raises an interesting question to those of us who are more familiar with what the Americans call the Nordic type of beauty. It seems that Mr. Hoppé is asking a little too much of us when he asks admiration for Indian, Hawaiian, and Chinese beauties. There may be Venuses among the Hottentots, but it must either be a very educated palate that appreciates them, or people capable of blinding themselves to the national distaste for colour. Mr. Hoppé's book raises the question: Is it possible for a coloured woman to be beautiful?'[43]

Most reviewers were far more circumspect, although few could resist the temptation to tally the results of Hoppé's deliberations. 'Fairest Women Picked' screamed the headline in the *Seattle Washington Times,* 'America Given Six, Princess White Deer, Indian, Among Them'.[44] *Drawing* magazine declared that the book would 'delight the soul of any artist',[45] *Home* described it as a book 'every one will want to possess',[46] and *Country Life,* noting that it 'exhibits humanity through the camera', described it as 'beautiful', and 'excellent'.[47] Already famous, Hoppé's exploits were reported with increasing fervour, becoming fodder for editorials and comic strips, such as 'Dorothy Darnit' (above).

Wherever he travelled, Hoppé was bombarded with requests to judge beauty pageants or organise party games to decide the most beautiful woman present. He received fan letters and hate mail from people who agreed with his selections or lamented the exclusion of their favourite candidate.[48]

Amid the furore stirred up by the book, its central innovation was lost. European art had long held a special place for 'exotic' beauties, but they were typically highly sexualised, as in Lucien Gauthier's photographs of Tahitian women made around the same time (right). Hoppé, by comparison, usually showed women clothed and tightly cropped, with their legs and torsos largely invisible. Edited this way, they fit comfortably with the format of other Hoppé types. More importantly, they reinforced his message that women are most beautiful when they realise their intellectual potential. In the context of the women's suffrage movements of the early twentieth century, this nuanced conception of beauty was meaningful.

Hoppé held that to be truly attractive, women must be thinking, striving and active individuals. This was the same standard to which he held flower sellers and charwomen — the idle rich held little appeal for him. He passed over candidates with merely pretty faces and figures, in favour of women who were socially engaged, employed as novelists, actresses and philanthropists. It may be a cliché, but his experience photographing at all wavelengths of the social spectrum had taught him not to judge people merely by the way they look. 'A rather firm conviction that there lies hid in the core of average humanity something much finer and nobler than appears on the surface predisposes me to look unceasingly for that inner beauty which reflects the personality far more truly than the form of structural arrangement of the features.'[49]

It was a philosophy forged in countless portrait sessions with sitters who were completely anonymous, and others among the most recognisable alive. 'Curiously enough,' Hoppé wrote, 'coincident in my interest in this search for beauty has been the discovery of certain qualifications within myself conducive to success. Sometimes a man or woman will enter my studio for the first time and I experience a mental thrill at their sheer beauty before I have time to observe their facial contours. It may be the intellectual loveliness of a finely strung mind which superimposes itself, it may be a dominating brain, the spirituality of the dreamer and visionary, or a lofty and noble character have invested the lineaments with a peculiar beauty, discernible by the mind, rather than the eye. The tenderness of love, the joy of living, a spirit mischievous and gay, may all contribute to an external and internal comeliness. Just as the plate in my camera is sensitive to light, so my brain seems to have developed a sensitivity to those with whom I come in contact.'[50] With this epiphany, forged equally in the studio and on the street, Hoppé had himself achieved a kind of perfection.

Hoppé spent decades trying to understand the complex interplay of personality and type. Although he was never able to mould his observations into a single cohesive theory, his investigations shaped every picture he made. Rarely did he simply depress the shutter release, relying on the camera to capture a subject. To Hoppé, people were more than a collection of physical characteristics. The act of photographing was never casual; it represented an intimate exchange from sitter to artist to viewer. In grappling with what makes certain individuals beautiful, Hoppé considered how personality may be manifest in appearance. In wrestling with questions of occupation, race and social standing, he tried to find those qualities that transcend historical circumstance or genetics. It was arguably this insistent drive not just to record, but to transmit his appreciation for sitters that makes his photographs distinctive. And it was his determination to distil the essence of personality – what we are, who we are, and how we got that way – that makes them so affecting.

Tahitian Beauty by Lucien Gauthier, *c*.1915

Notes

1   E.O. Hoppé, manuscript for an unpublished autobiography, E.O. Hoppé Estate Collection 0967-0001, n.d. (after 1964), p.5.
2   Ibid.
3   E.O. Hoppé, *Hundred Thousand Exposures* (London: Focal Press, 1945), pp.77–80.
4   Ibid.
5   Ibid.
6   Ibid.
7   Ibid.
8   Ibid., p.45.
9   Alyson Wilson, 'Housed in Art History', *Art Quarterly*, Spring 1994, p.24. '... the young Ellen Terry had been photographed on the balcony of Sir Coutts Lindsay's house opposite in 1864 by Julia Margaret Cameron ...'.
10 Bill Jay, *E.O. Hoppé 1878–1972: A Personal Snapshot* (unpublished essay, 1981), p.1.
11 Cecil Beaton, 'Presenting a Master of the Camera', in E.O. Hoppé, 1945, op. cit., p.5.
12 Ibid.
13 E.O. Hoppé, *A Study of Ethnography on London's Pavements*, E.O. Hoppé Estate Collection 0988, n.d., p.1.
14 Ibid., p.4.
15 References to husbands nominating their wives for Hoppé's recognition appear repeatedly in newspaper accounts of the time. See also E.O. Hoppé, 1945, op. cit., p.97.
16 J.D. Beresford and E.O. Hoppé, *Taken from Life* (London: Collins), 1922, p.217.
17 E.O. Hoppé, 1945, op. cit., p.28.
18 Ibid.
19 In Baroque Flemish and Dutch art, for example, the practice of producing anonymous portrait heads or 'tronies' typifying certain personality types was common; in the eighteenth century, Johann Kaspar Lavater promulgated theories of personality based on physiognomy in his influential *Physiognomische Fragmente* (1775–8). There are many other examples one could point to, before and since.
20 August Sander, *Antlitz der Zeit*, (Munich: Transmare/Kurt Wolff, 1929).
21 E.O. Hoppé, manuscript for an unpublished autobiography, E.O. Hoppé Estate Collection 0187, n.d., p.6.
22 E.O. Hoppé, manuscript for an unpublished autobiography, E.O. Hoppé Estate Collection 0221, n.d., p. 8.
23 E.O. Hoppé, 'G.B.S.' E.O. Hoppé Estate Collection, n.d., unnumbered note.
24 E.O. Hoppé, 1945, op. cit., p.90.
25 Ibid.
26 Ibid.
27 'Fashions in Beards from Many Lands', *Sunday Express,* 24 November 1929, unpaginated. E.O. Hoppé Estate Collection 1486.
28 E.O. Hoppé, manuscript for an unpublished autobiography, E.O. Hoppé Estate Collection 0221, n.d., p.8.
29 Stacy Aumonier, *Odd Fish: Being a Casual Selection of London Residents Described and Drawn* (London: Heinemann, 1923).
30 J.D Beresford and E.O. Hoppé, 1922, op. cit., pp.127–8.
31 Ibid., p.140.
32 E.O. Hoppé, 'G.B.S.' E.O. Hoppé Estate Collection, n.d., unnumbered note.
33 E.O. Hoppé, 'George Bernard Shaw' unpublished manuscript, E.O. Hoppé Estate Collection 0182, n.d., pp.4–5.
34 Ibid., p.4.
35 Ibid.
36 E.O. Hoppé, 'G. B. Shaw – brilliant' E.O. Hoppé Estate Collection, n.d., unnumbered note.
37 E.O. Hoppé, manuscript for an unpublished autobiography, E.O. Hoppé Estate Collection 1078-0002, n.d. (after 1964), p.7.
38 E.O. Hoppé, manuscript for an unpublished autobiography, E.O. Hoppé Estate Collection 0221, n.d. (after 1964), p.81.
39 *Graphic*, 9 January, 1932, pp.44–5.
40 Russell Roberts, *Tony Ray-Jones* (Bradford: National Museum of Photography, Film, and Television, 2004), pp.145–50.
41 Ray-Jones, writing in *Creative Camera*, 1968, as cited in Roberts, 2004, op. cit., cover and p.13.
42 E.O. Hoppé, 'The Rhythm of Perfect Types' E.O. Hoppé Estate Collection 0985, unpublished manuscript, p.2.
43 'Are There Black Beauties?', *Scarborough Post,* 26 October 1922, unpaginated, E.O. Hoppé Estate Collection 0995-0010.
44 'Fairest Women Picked', *Seattle Washington Post,* 26 November 1922, unpaginated, Hoppé Archive 0995.
45 'Types of Beauty', *Drawing,* December 1922, pp.276–7, E.O. Hoppé Estate Collection 0995-003.
46 'The Books of 1922', *Home,* December 1922, unpaginated. E.O. Hoppé Estate Collection 0995-0016.
47 *Country Life,* 9 December 1922, p.777, E.O. Hoppé Estate Collection 0995-0027.
48 The E.O. Hoppé Estate Collection hold examples of these letters.
49 E.O. Hoppé, 'Beauty and Personality' unpublished manuscript, E.O. Hoppé Estate Collection 0967-0001, p.2.
50 Ibid., pp.2–3. Punctuation edited.

E.O. HOPPÉ
A BIOGRAPHY

Terence Pepper

Emil Otto Hoppé was born in Munich on 14 April 1878, son of Philipp Hoppé, a bank director, and his wife, Marie von der Porter, a pianist. Soon after his birth the family moved to Vienna, where Hoppé began his formal education, which he later completed in Paris and Munich.[1] Although his ambition was to be a painter and graphic artist, Hoppé was persuaded by his father to enter the family profession of banking, and went, without much enthusiasm, into the bank of which his father was a director. However, at weekends he attended art classes at the studio of the Munich watercolourist Hans von Bartels. After a year, it became obvious that he had little aptitude for banking, and it was decided that he should go to work for his uncle, head of a firm of export merchants in Shanghai. Around 1902, on their way east, Hoppé and his uncle stopped in London, where the latter had business to transact. Hoppé decided not to continue his journey, and with his uncle's help obtained a post with the Deutsche Bank, located at 4 George Yard, Lombard Street in the City of London.[2]

In London Hoppé encountered the well-known amateur photographer J.C. Warburg and was so impressed with the fine results he achieved, and with the creative possibilities of photography, that he bought his first camera, a Goerz-Anschütz. In November 1903 Hoppé, then living in Clifton Gardens in Maida Vale, London, applied to and was elected a member of the Royal Photographic Society (RPS), then the leading society for aspirant amateur photographers whose work could be submitted for exhibition at their annual photographic salon.[3] He was particularly helped and encouraged by several key photographers and photo-editors of the time that he met at the society, such as (John) Furley Lewis (later President of the RPS), H. Snowden Ward, editor of *Photographic Monthly* and *Photograms of the Year*, the American-born Alvin Langdon Coburn, whose subject matter and publications would closely foreshadow Hoppé's, and the Reverend F.C. Lambert, editor of the journal *Practical Photographer*.[4]

By 1905, for exhibiting purposes, he had changed his name from Emil to E.O. Hoppé, possibly following the fashionable trend of having a two-letter forename abbreviation such as A.L. Coburn, H.G. Ponting, J.C. Warburg, G.C. Beresford and E.H. Mills, or, possibly, to distance himself from his contemporary, Austrian architect, Emil Hoppé. Now living at 12 Ranelagh Avenue in Barnes, London, Hoppé had his first two photographs accepted to be shown at the RPS Salon and became a regular and successful entrant to photographic exhibitions and competitions.[5] In the same year, at the age of twenty-seven, Hoppé married the twenty-four-year-old Marion Josephine Wilhelmina Bliersbach. Between 1911 and 1916 Marion ran a fashionable dressmakers, Marion Hoppé et Cie, near Portman Square,[6] which was to provide a measure of financial security as her husband established himself.

E.O. Hoppé by Rudolf Dührkoop, 1909

Hoppé had nine more works selected for exhibition at the fifty-first and fifty-second RPS Annual Exhibitions shown at the New Gallery in Regent Street in 1906 and 1907. In 1906 these included his portrait of his friend A.L. Coburn, whose career and one-man show that year were being publicised by George Bernard Shaw, two narrative portraits, *The Critic* and *The Visitor*, as well as a portrait of Cecil Heywood. In 1907 his genre study, *An Auld Licht*, and two celebrity sitters, the war correspondent Mario Fortini and his fellow photographer, H. Snowden Ward, were among five chosen for exhibition.[7] These early exhibits of typologies and character portraits of well-known personalities were to mark Hoppé's twin interests throughout his career.

After winning various photographic competitions Hoppé gave up his bank job to become a professional photographer.[8] He opened his first studio at 10 Margravine Gardens on 1 October 1907.[9] Margravine Gardens was a quiet residential street that had acquired a faintly bohemian air from the number of artists living and working there. In unpublished autobiographical notes Hoppé remarks, 'I found an attractive little house with a large studio at Baron's Court which lies between the borderline of aristocratic South and genteel West Kensington ... The studio was on the second floor and was reached from below by a quaint wooden staircase ... there was no skylight but this did not bother me ... Margravine Gardens was one of a row of artists' dwellings, most occupied by young painters.'[10] Hoppé's house had previously belonged to the illustrator and Royal Academician Arthur Garrett. It was here that Hoppé held weekly informal gatherings of artists and photographers. On some of these lively evenings, Herbert Ponting, later official photographer on Robert Falcon Scott's Antarctic expedition, sang while Hoppé accompanied him on the guitar. Hoppé's Christmas card from 1907, which reproduced a photograph by Furley Lewis,[11] shows him and Marion in the artistically decorated studio-drawing room at Margravine Gardens. The photograph is displayed within a decorative surround that alludes to the Vienna Secession motif of framing by two bay trees (below).

What Next, 1910
E.O Hoppé's pictorial narrative portrait was exhibited as a planiotype print at the Annual Exhibition of the Royal Photographic Society in 1910.

Marion and E.O. Hoppé's Christmas card, 1907

In November 1907, a month after opening his studio, Hoppé was elected as a Fellow of the Royal Photographic Society (FRPS). His reputation in photographic circles was growing and he was frequently in demand as a lecturer and writer on photography.[12] In 1909 he was chosen, along with Sir Benjamin Stone, to organise the British contribution to the Dresden International Exhibition of Photography, whose specially built galleries cost over £4,000 and covered more than 1½ acres.[13] The exhibition ran from May to October. Hoppé was in charge of hanging and arranging the pictorial work of British photographers such as F.H. Evans, Frederick Hollyer and Cavendish Morton, as well as some of his own recent portraits, while Stone was responsible for record photographs.[14] Elsewhere the International Group of Art Photographers exhibited in their own Hall of Honour, which included 244 works by eighteen photographers. The works were mainly from members of the association of photographers called the Linked Ring, including large numbers of prints by Edward Steichen (thirty), Alfred Stieglitz (fourteen) and A.L. Coburn (seventeen), with the Americans dominating and provoking a critical backlash. Although Hoppé was to be nominated for membership of the prestigious Linked Ring in 1909, the group, which started in 1892 after seceding from the RPS, broke up before he could join.[15] Hoppé was, however, to be one of the founders of its successor, the London Salon of Photography, in 1910. While in Dresden, Hoppé took the opportunity of photographing a number of European celebrities and heads of state, including Ludwig, Prince Regent of Bavaria.[16]

Mrs Alec Tweedie, 1910

Hoppé in Print

Back in London his enhanced position led to the start of a series of regular commissions for leading magazines of the era, known colloquially as the 'Great Eight'. These included: the *Illustrated London News*, the *Graphic*, the *Sphere*, the *Tatler*, the *Sketch,* the *Illustrated Sporting and Dramatic News* and the *Bystander*. Hoppé's first full-page reproduction was commissioned by the *Bystander* in 1909, a portrait of Lord Curzon, former Viceroy of India.[17] Several of these large-format titles started in the Edwardian age and provided a forum for spectacular photographs that could, for the first time, be reproduced by the half-tone printing process, rather than appearing as line engravings based on photographs, as they had done previously. Hoppé's second commission for the *Bystander,* a portrait of the actor-manager Sir Herbert Beerbohm Tree, was one of the first to appear with the block-letter titling that became the signature style for a lot of his works created between 1909 and 1911. This reflected the fashion of the time and the style of the high-art photographers whose work appeared in Alfred Steiglitz's serial publication *Camera Work*. Two examples, such as his studies of Philip Snowden, Chancellor of the Exchequer, and the important woman travel writer, Mrs Alec Tweedie, show Hoppé's design and graphic art skills combined. Hoppé's signature appears in the plate, together with the date and Secessionist lettering to complete the composition (right).

Most of Hoppé's sitters were sufficiently well known for their portraits to be in demand by the press, and he relied on reproduction fees as much as on the sale of prints for his income. The work of Hoppé and his contemporary photographers, such as Malcolm Arbuthnot, Bertram Park and Hugh Cecil, was of a strikingly elevated standard, and the status of portrait photography immediately before and during the First World War was higher than it had been for a long time. Reproductions in magazines and periodicals reflected this, being of superb technical quality. Photographs were usually described as 'camera portraits' or 'camera studies' to emphasise their artistic merits, and the photographer, or 'camera artist', insisted on being named so that each reproduction acted as an advertisement. From the beginning of his career,

ALL SORTS AND CONDITIONS OF MEN: CAMERA-PICTURES BY HOPPE.

PORTRAITS EXHIBITED AT THE ONE-MAN SHOW AT THE ROYAL PHOTOGRAPHIC SOCIETY'S.

1. A GREAT TENOR: SIGNOR CARUSO.   3. A GREAT ACTOR: SIR HERBERT TREE.
3. A GREAT DIPLOMATIST: LORD CURZON OF KEDLESTON.   4. A GREAT AMBASSADOR: HIS EXCELLENCY LI-CHING-FONG.

Page featuring photographs by E.O. Hoppé from his first one-man show at the RPS, *Illustrated London News*, 9 April 1910.

Hoppé had been on friendly terms with Dr Bulloch and Bruce Ingram, editors respectively of the *Graphic* and the *Illustrated London News*, and from 1909 onwards they not only published his portraits but also regularly commissioned him to photograph eminent personalities.[18]

In April 1910 Hoppé held his first one-man show at the RPS. This consisted of seventy-two photographs and received much favourable publicity, particularly in the *Illustrated London News*, which published sixteen of the portraits, including those of painter and etcher, William Strang (p.87), Sir Herbert Beerbohm Tree, Imperial Chinese Ambassador Li-Ching-Fong, painter Frank Brangwyn and opera singer Enrico Caruso, in a four-page supplement (above). This in particular helped to bring Hoppé's name to the attention of the general public, and during the next decade he was to become one of the best-known and most successful London portraitists. Hoppé was commissioned by the *Graphic* to do a series of great men of the day, which were published at full-page size, 16 x 11 inches. These included photographs of European diplomats such as the Austro-Hungarian ambassador Count Mensdorff-Pouilly and the Prussian and German ambassador to London Count Paul-Wolff Metternich, and prominent playwrights and artists such as Arthur Wing Pinero and Royal Academician James Sant.[19]

Baker Street and the Russian Ballet

In February 1911 Hoppé moved to a larger and more central studio at 59 Baker Street. Here he did an increasing amount of theatrical photography, some for the Court Theatre which, under the management of Harley Granville-Barker and J.E. Vedrenne, was introducing new plays by George Bernard Shaw and Henrik Ibsen to London audiences, often with stage designs by Edward Gordon Craig (p.62).[20] Hoppé was commissioned to design the souvenir anniversary programmes for two successful musicals produced by the impresario George Edwardes: Oscar Straus's *The Chocolate Soldier* and Leo Fall's *The Dollar Princess*. For the stage director Max Reinhardt (p.60) he photographed the principal actors in *The Miracle*, one of the most spectacular theatrical events of the era, as well as *Sumurun*, which featured Clotilde von Derp (p.55), and in collaboration with Malcolm Arbuthnot, *Oedipus Rex*. As early as 1909 he had photographed Ruth St Denis and was to return to photograph her and her dance company partner, Ted Shawn, on many occasions up until their 1920s performances, including the modernistic costumed *Tillers of the Soil* (1922) (pp.44, 54).[21]

But it is for his photographs of the Russian Ballet company, brought to Britain by Serge Diaghilev, that Hoppé has become best remembered. Hoppé, who recalled meeting Diaghilev in Moscow as well at von Bartels's Munich studio in 1894, secured the exclusive rights to photograph the leading members of the Ballet when the troupe first came to London in June 1911, and co-hosted two receptions at his studio with the dancer Tamara Karsavina (right, pp.49, 52). The company caused a sensation, and Léon Bakst's costume and stage designs set a new fashion in clothes and decoration (p.48). Hoppé's photographs of the dancers Karsavina, Bolm and Fokine managed to evoke this exotic colour and spectacle, and attracted considerable public interest (pp.51, 53). Eighteen of his *Studies from the Russian Ballet* were included in an exhibition of his work at the Goupil Gallery, Regent Street, in February 1913, and thirteen were published in a portfolio of gravures by the Fine Art Society.[22] The latter also included two earlier studies of Nijinsky in costume for von Weber's *Le Spectre de la Rose* and as the Golden Slave in Rimsky-Korsakov's *Scheherazade* by French photographer Auguste Bert, taken in Paris against a painted backdrop. The set of gravures, which represented Hoppé's first book, appeared in different printed folders, with some later copies omitting Bert's name from the cover credit and thereby causing confusion to some over the authorship of the images of Nijinsky. Hoppé did eventually persuade Nijinsky to be photographed by him backstage in London in a study that currently enjoys his highest price for a portrait sold at auction (p.47).[23] The Goupil Gallery exhibition also included some of his most powerful literary portraits, such as those of Rudyard Kipling and Henry James, Arnold Bennett in profile holding a cigarette (regarded by Cecil Beaton as one of Hoppé's best portraits – opposite), and the futurist F.T. Marinetti, which Hoppé later combined with his own futuristic notes and drawings to suggest a double exposure (pp.78, 92, 98).

Millais House

Hoppé, who was becoming one of the best known and most successful portrait photographers in London, felt it was time to expand his business once more. He leased 7 Cromwell Place, a large terraced house in an imposing and wealthy residential area near the Victoria and Albert Museum in South Kensington,

Tamara Karsavina as the Firebird, 1911, one of the gravure plates from *Studies from the Russian Ballet* (published 1913).

London. Conveniently placed for prospective clients, the street also had a certain artistic cachet: at number 5 lived the fashionable society portrait painter John Lavery, and Hoppé's own house had belonged to Sir John Everett Millais from 1861 to 1877. Lewis Carroll had visited it in 1865 to photograph Millais and his family and, in 1864, Julia Margaret Cameron had photographed Ellen Terry at Sir Coutts Lindsay's house opposite. In 1900 Terry was painted as Shakespeare's heroine Imogen by Mrs Margaret Cookesley,[24] and in 1919 sat for Hoppé in costume as the nurse from *Romeo and Juliet* in the same studio (p.63).

Hoppé renamed 7 Cromwell Place 'Millais House' for his studio stamp and made good use of the ample space for living accommodation, darkrooms, storage areas and studios. Hoppé gave much thought to the decoration of the public rooms, knowing that the impression these made would affect the atmosphere of the sittings themselves. He described the sybaritic splendour of the main reception room in his autobiography: 'The walls were black with a relief design of clover purple and jade. Heavy shot green and gold curtains with a deep purple carpet defined the colour scheme, and a scarlet and gold table centred in the middle of the room.'[25] The dressing-rooms, essential when sitters brought changes of clothes with them or wished to be photographed in fancy-dress, were decorated in orange tussore silk.

Millais' own studio was used by Hoppé for his photography, and, prizing its artistic associations, he changed it as little as possible. The walls were covered in unbleached cloth, the polished floor left bare except for a few Persian rugs. The furnishings were carefully chosen, partly for their intrinsic beauty and partly for their usefulness as props: a grand piano, a tapestry hanging, a Chinese gold-leaf screen, a carved chair, busts by Jacob Epstein (p.81) and Ivan Mestrovic, the two leading sculptors that Hoppé had photographed in addition to artistically photographing their work.[26] As far as possible, the atmosphere was that of a restful and informal drawing-room. The camera was a specially designed 10 x 8 inch reflex, made to be as unobtrusive as possible and to eliminate any necessity for the photographer to dive under yards of black cloth, an activity that had hitherto detracted from his personal dignity. For lighting, Hoppé installed little more than two floodlights and a spotlight, his bulky artificial lighting equipment being concentrated in a studio elsewhere in the house.

Hoppé maintained that the technical process of photography should be as simple as possible so that the photographer could be free to establish rapport with his sitter. He relied on his studio's restful atmosphere and on his own confident, unhurried and friendly manner to put the sitter at ease. He was genuinely interested in his sitters and made it his business to be well informed on a wide range of topics so that he could converse easily with the variety of people who came to be photographed. As he talked with them, he studied them, watching for expressions or gestures that he felt to be natural or characteristic. He then used a cable-release to operate the shutter as unobtrusively as possible.

After his move to Millais House and the birth of his two children, Frank Sidney and Muriel Marion,[27] Hoppé was much more in demand as a chronicler of society beauties and stage stars from the hit musical comedies of the day, such as Regine Flory, Gaby Deslys and Gina Palerme (pp.66–7). His work was perhaps most in demand for the *Sketch*, the *Tatler*, the *Bystander* and *Eve*, which reflected the popular interest in the stage and society. Throughout the war years, an increasing number of Hoppé's pictures were published. In 1913 the *Tatler* published only thirty of his portraits, but by 1915 this number had grown to 115, and by 1917 to over 150. During 1917 Hoppé photographed 665 sitters, the largest number for any year of his career.

Arnold Bennett, 1911

In 1916 Hoppé began to undertake fashion photography for the retailer D.H. Evans, and also for Lucile, the fashion house owned by Lady Duff-Gordon. He photographed Lucile's most famous model, Constance Vesselier, who the couturier named 'Hebe' – an image that was later to appear in Hoppé's *Book of Fair Women* (p.41).[28] Some of Hoppé's society portraits had been published in the American edition of *Vogue* magazine and when the British edition was launched in September 1916 he took many of the editorial photographs for the first few issues, including a study of Lady Lavery for the inaugural issue. Although Baron de Meyer, with his more dramatic effects, soon took over as the main *Vogue* photographer, Hoppé continued for some time to contribute to the magazine, and also to *Vanity Fair,* the other Condé Nast title. *Vanity Fair*, which had a particular interest in publishing and commissioning portraits of iconic figures in the arts, published Hoppé's portraits of Henry James in 1913 (p.98), Thomas Hardy in 1914 (p.93), and in October 1921 he photographed Willa Cather for the magazine in New York.[29] One of the last issues of *Vanity Fair* before its closure in 1936 featured a full-page reproduction of Hoppé's study *The Fisherman*.[30]

Early in his career, Hoppé had photographed writers such as Jerome K. Jerome, H. Rider Haggard and Arnold Bennett. Arthur St John Adcock, editor of *Bookman*, had seen and published these portraits, and offered Hoppé a long-term contract to take the portraits needed to illustrate the monthly issues and the specially enlarged annual Christmas editions, which included full page gravure reproductions of subjects such as the poet Edward Thomas (p.103). Hoppé's portraits were also widely published in American magazines, including the deluxe photographic art magazine *Shadowland*, which featured his stage, cinema, literary and music portrait subjects, such as his December 1919 sitting with the poet T.S. Eliot and his May 1920 sitting with the composer Ralph Vaughan Williams.

In addition to photographs, Hoppé produced drawings and woodcuts based on his photographs of, for example, Rudyard Kipling. Those of John Masefield and Thomas Hardy, whose photographic portraits were reproduced in *Bookman* in 1913 and 1914 respectively, were published as woodblock prints in December 1925. He also made literary contributions, such as an article describing his visit to photograph the poet and dramatist Maurice Maeterlinck at his home in Ghent[31] and in early 1924 an extensive article on George Bernard Shaw, after visiting him at his home in Adelphi Terrace (pp.114–15).[32] Hoppé's collaboration with St John Adcock also resulted in the publication of two books of literary biography and portraits, *Gods of Modern Grub Street* (1923) and *The Glory that Was Grub Street* (1928). In a similar format, Hoppé's collection of photographs of American writers, taken in New York in November 1926, included Robert Frost, Eugene O'Neill and Willa Cather, with text by Elizabeth Sergeant and was published, by Alfred A. Knopf, in New York in 1927.[33]

At the end of 1921 Hoppé was invited to Buckingham Palace to photograph King George V, and in December the following year he was invited to photograph Queen Mary. His studies of the King and Queen were unusually informal in comparison with their other official portraits of the time. The King was pictured at work at his desk (p.107), while the Queen was photographed both at her writing desk and beside a cabinet of jade objects, as if showing her prized collection to an interested visitor. Hoppé's portraits of the King became some of the most iconic of his reign and reappeared in various forms over the following years in colourised versions, culminating in a painted version by Bernard Munns, which formed a double-page supplement in the Christmas 1928 edition of *Illustrated London News*. Queen Mary's portraits similarly enjoyed a long currency and appeared on the 22 May 1937 cover of *Weekly Illustrated* (above) to celebrate her seventieth birthday and to show her welcoming the

E.O Hoppé's photograph of Queen Mary, taken in 1922, on the cover of *Weekly Illustrated*, 22 May 1937.

Coronation of her son George VI and his consort Queen Elizabeth. Hoppé had photographed the new royal couple as the Duke and Duchess of York in April 1923 and the Duchess alone (pp.108–9), having first photographed her as the teenage Lady Elizabeth Bowes-Lyon in 1914.

The Book of Fair Women
The publication that caused the most press interest and that has continued to fascinate since it came out in 1922 is *The Book of Fair Women*. It was published in a limited edition of 560 numbered copies, first in Britain and then in America and Germany.[34] It contained thirty-two photogravure plates of his portraits of beautiful women from around the world and did more than anything else to consolidate his reputation as a connoisseur of female beauty. The German edition had four additional plates, taken by the daughter of Hoppé's friend and mentor, the leading German portraitist Rudolf Dührkoop, Minya Diez-Dührkoop who had worked with her father and carried on his business. The origins of Hoppé's selection can be traced back to a feature published in *Bystander* in 1913 entitled 'Which Nation Has the Best Sitters? Types from the Portfolio of a Camera Portraitist' followed by a Hoppé quote from the *Pall Mall Gazette*, 'I have photographed Spanish women, Italian women, French women, very many Russian women, Austrian women, Swedish, Norwegian, and American women. And I have no hesitation whatever in saying that to me the most interesting sitter is the Englishwoman.'[35]

Sir John and Lady Lavery, photographed for the catalogue of their joint exhibition at the Alpine Club Gallery, 1921.

The article itself only compares Spanish against English types, but is symptomatic of a perennial press interest in differing international perceptions of beauty. Although some of the subjects were certainly photographed for the book, a considerable number of plates go back to sittings in 1911 and 1915, thus producing a useful career overview of 'fair women' sitters. Images from 1921 include Mrs Tokugawa and Madame Wellington Koo (p.34). In 1920 the *New York Times* announced that Hoppé had arrived in the United States on the *Caronia* to seek five 'American beauties' to match the 'Belles of England'.[36] His photographs of the film stars Anna Q. Nilsson and Marion Davies (p.68) were both taken in New York that year.

Two of the portraits included in *The Book of Fair Women* show subjects in historical costume and reflect a larger body of Hoppé's work, which recorded the elaborate theatre tableaux of the period, staged for the war effort and posed by leading members of society. Hoppé's photograph of Viscountess Massereene and Ferrard shows her in the guise of a painting of Beatrice d'Este *c*.1490 (p.42). The image first appeared as a double-page spread in the *Tatler*, on 17 January 1917, on the occasion of her performance in an Italian masque given in aid of His Majesty's Prisoners of War Fund. Lady Lavery is depicted in costume 'after Holbein' in a photograph that was first published in the *Tatler* on 27 June 1917 (p.42), along with two variant poses with text giving details of her forthcoming appearance in the Swinburne Ballet at the Coliseum in aid of the Concerts at the Front Fund.[37] Lady Lavery and her husband (right) lived opposite Hoppé at 5 Cromwell Place and she was one of Hoppé's most photographed subjects, posing again in costume as Bouguereau's *Vierge Consolatrice* with Violet de Trafford as 'the fallen woman', a role that both Lady Diana Manners and Nancy Cunard had declined (p.79).[38]

The Book of Fair Women belongs to a sub-genre of photographic surveys that also includes Bassano's *England's Beautiful Women* of 1909, Hugh Cecil's similarly formatted book of gravures, *A Book of Beauty* (1927), and Cecil Beaton's first publication, *The Book of Beauty* (1930), which combined his drawings and photographs. Hoppé's book is particular in its ethnographic approach, selecting thirty-two representative beauties from twenty-four different countries. Hoppé was often asked to name his most beautiful sitters, but diplomatically refused to do so until he had closed his studio. He then said that the actresses Lady Diana Cooper (p.43), Gladys Cooper (below) and the model Hebe had been his favourite English sitters, while Marion Davies and Lady Lavery were the loveliest American women he had ever photographed.[39]

Hoppé and the Arts

Throughout his career Hoppé became involved with many and various artistic activities. After the First World War, for instance, he founded the Dorien Leigh Galleries, first in Bruton Street, London and, after a year, in Millais House itself. Using Dorien Leigh as a pseudonym, Hoppé provided facilities for exhibiting a wide range of pure and applied arts, from Danish furniture and silver to the stage designs of Gordon Craig and Herman Rosse. In 1921 Hoppé exhibited the work of, among others, Russian-born painter Max Weber and fourteen-year-old Stephen Tennant. It was reported that Queen Alexandra visited the Tennant show and bought a work entitled *The Boy who Saw the Fairies*.[40] Subsequently, the Dorien Leigh Gallery played host to Maxwell Armfield (1922) and Gluck, whose first London exhibition was held there in 1924 (p.88). Hoppé's own designs for silks and lacquers formed part of one of the first exhibitions organised by the Decorative Arts Group, whose aim was to educate the public to be aware of good design in everyday objects. In 1913, one of Hoppé's modish drawings appeared in the *Tatler*, revealing the flair for design and composition that were his chief strengths as a photographer. He wrote many articles for arts magazines, such as *Drawing and Design*, *Commercial Art* and *Studio*, and was also a contributing editor of *Artwork*, but the journal with which he was most closely associated was *Colour*. In January 1914 discussions were held at Millais House about the launching of this new monthly, to be 'devoted to colour, strength and vitality in art and literature'.[41] It would feature articles on interesting developments in contemporary arts, short stories of a high literary quality and colour reproductions of important new paintings. Financial backing was provided by Lord Leverhulme, the millionaire soap manufacturer and philanthropist who had founded Port Sunlight, and the journal was edited by Alfred Wilson Barrett and the novelist Charles Marriott. Hoppé was to be art editor, contributing articles and reviews on photographic subjects, as well as

Two plates from *The Book of Fair Women*:
left, Gladys Cooper, 1921
right, Madame Wellington Koo, 1921

some of his own drawings and fabric designs. Other contributors included the artists Augustus John, George Clausen, Harold Gilman, Paul Nash and the writer Eden Phillpotts, and although the first issue inauspiciously coincided with the outbreak of the First World War, *Colour* continued publication until the 1930s.

In 1917 Hoppé made Millais House available as the headquarters of The Plough, a private theatrical group whose aim was to produce plays 'new and original in conception' that 'had not previously been performed in England'.[42] Fellow committee members included A.L. Coburn, dramatist Clifford Bax and his brother, composer Arnold Bax, Jacob Epstein, Lady Lavery, architect Charles Rennie Mackintosh, painter Glyn Philpot and artist George Sheringham. During the two years of its existence, The Plough, financed by the subscriptions of its members, put on several plays. Hoppé himself helped with the scenery and designed sets for some of the productions.[43] He was to have produced the group's first film, but unfortunately The Plough broke up before this could be made, mainly because of its members' commitments elsewhere.

Round the World with a Camera

The turning point for Hoppé's career as a portrait photographer came in 1922 when his largest-ever one-man exhibition, with 221 exhibits, opened on 5 January at the Goupil Gallery. In addition to 134 portraits of identified subjects, the exhibition included London and New York types, still lifes, views of New York, and a selection from *The Book of Fair Women*.[44] The introduction to the catalogue was written by the novelist and playwright John Galsworthy, whose text concentrated on the section of 'human documents' included in the show. The exhibition received favourable reviews: *Manchester Dispatch* called Hoppé 'the Sargent of the camera', while the *Observer* predicted that his portraits of 'Galsworthy, Henry James and the like would remain a record of the age' and the reviewer in *Truth* praised his abilities as a 'keen psychologist and bold designer.' *Ideal Home* took a strictly practical viewpoint, pronouncing the portraits 'ideally adapted to decorate the modern home'.[45] After the exhibition had toured Britain, it was bought in its entirety by the Asahi Shimbun Company of Tokyo, a Japanese photographic collection. During Hoppé's fifteen years as a professional photographer he had focused almost exclusively on studio portraiture, and he now wanted to explore the fresh creative possibilities of other types of photography. Although he maintained his Millais House studio until 1937, taking some fine portraits during these years, much of his later work was devoted to travel and photographic essays.

Some of his best work in the 1920s was taken abroad. Between 1919 and 1921, and in 1926, at the suggestion of the entrepreneur Al Woods, Hoppé spent some four months each year operating a portrait studio on 57th Street, New York. Here he photographed Charles Dana Gibson (creator of the iconic 'Gibson Girl'). He was commissioned by Dr Bulloch, the editor of the *Graphic* to photograph the fascist dictator Mussolini in 1924 (p.111) and he also made several trips to Germany between 1927 and 1929. In Berlin in 1927 he took portraits of German cultural figures, including writer Lion Feuchtwanger, editor of *Berliner Illustrirte Zeitung* Kurt Korff, composer Siegfried Ochs and conductor Bruno Walter. In 1928 and 1929 he photographed stars for the Ufa Film Studios, including the director of *Metropolis* Fritz Lang and the film's leading lady, Brigitte Helm (pp.70–1). Hoppé's images of stars filming in Berlin, including the British-born Lilian Harvey, Lya De Putti, Leni Riefenstahl and Dita Parlo (p.36), were also published in the prestigious and highly collectable Ross Verlag series of postcards with the credit 'Camera Portrait by E.O. Hoppé, London'.[46] During the latter half of the 1920s and throughout the 1930s Hoppé travelled to India, Ceylon (Sri Lanka), Australia, New Zealand and the Dutch East Indies (Indonesia).

Wherever he travelled, Hoppé made a special point of recording interesting faces, whether they were of Romanian peasants, Native Americans or Zulus in Africa. He had a particular interest in physiognomy, and had a friendly exchange of models with the *Punch* cartoonist George Belcher, who specialised in drawing Cockney characters. Hoppé's work in this genre – truthful and sympathetic photographs of charladies, flower-sellers, cabmen, tramps and vagrants – formed the basis for two more books, *Taken from Life* (1922) and *London Types* (1926). These are a remarkable contrast to the elegantly posed society portrait photographs that formed the basis for his reputation as a fashionable photographer.

During his travels Hoppé recorded his impressions of the countries he visited for a series of topographical books, among the best of which were those commissioned for the Orbis Terrarum series. Each contained about 300 plates reproduced in gravure in a rich sepia colour, with a short introductory text and captions in four languages. *Picturesque Great Britain* (1926) recorded the beauty and tranquillity of a traditional way of life being threatened by the movement of population to the cities, and *Romantic America* (1927) concentrated on the natural wonders and endless contrasts that Hoppé found in the American landscape. Another of his books in a similar format, *Deutsche Arbeit* (1930), reproduced a series of powerful photographs of German industry at work. His pictures of cranes, oil pipes and factory interiors are some of the most significant photographs of industrial landscapes of the late 1920s and early 1930s.

E.O. Hoppé's portrait of Dita Parlo reproduced as a postcard for the Ross Verlag series, 1929.

Photojournalism

From the early 1920s until the outbreak of the Second World War, in September 1939, Hoppé concentrated increasingly on the new field of photojournalism. His first press photograph had been taken during a portrait sitting with the Prince of Nepal at the Franco-British Exhibition at White City in London in August 1908. The image, of the effects of a fatal gas explosion of a large airship, was published in the *Daily Mirror*.[47] Hoppé's photojournalistic contributions appeared regularly in the *Graphic* between 1930 and 1932 (the year the magazine closed).[48] Two such stories were 'Photographing the Maharaja of Udaipur',[49] taken in India, where Hoppé was working with his son Frank, and, a fifteen-picture, three-page story entitled 'Training the Army Officer', which documented the daily routine of the 'gentleman cadet' training to fight for the Empire, and featured 'embryo officers' being dragged out of bed in their pyjamas, shaving, exercising, fencing, eating and on parade (pp.124, 127). The multi-racial members of the 'private wireless class' are shown studying in their striped blazers with the door in the background bearing the sign 'Television Room', reflecting the latest development in broadcast media five months before the first BBC television broadcast.[50] His 1931 double-page spread 'A Day in the Museums', featuring scenes in the Natural History Museum, was part of a larger portfolio of images taken in museums.[51] His studies of children at the British Museum would subsequently appear in *The Image of London* (1935), one of Hoppé's many books on London.

In 1933, Hoppé was in Austria taking an exclusive photo-reportage series of the Austrian dictator Dr Dollfuss, relaxing with his family at Wolfpassing for *Illustrated London News*.[52] Soon after, an attempt was made to assassinate Dollfuss and Hoppé's four-picture story became part of a more significant news item. Much of the pioneering work in photojournalism, which would replace the traditional type of picture magazine in Europe, occurred in Germany in magazines such as *Münchner Illustrierte Preße* and *Berliner Illustrirte Zeitung*, in which Hoppé's work was shown alongside other masters of the photo-essay, including James Abbe and Martin Munkácsi. Hoppé's encounter with a bear

Singing in chapel, Roedean
school, Brighton, 1935

in America featured on the cover of the Berlin magazine, whilst his portrait
of Anna May Wong was a cover of the Munich publication.[53]

Illustrated London News continued to publish Hoppé's work, most
notably his photo-essay on Roedean public school for girls in 1935 (above,
p.162), but the outlet for cutting-edge photojournalism was firstly Weekly
Illustrated and later Picture Post.[54] The former ran essays featuring Hoppés
behind-the-scenes pictures of Madame Tussaud's (p.153) and a back cover
feature of Hoppé's female types entitled 'Old Ladies', which reprised images
that had first appeared in earlier publications.

Hoppé also travelled outside London. On a trip to Devon and Cornwall
with John Betjeman in 1932 he took photographs of old sea-farers at the
sixteenth-century Jolly Sailor's Inn, West Looe and location portraits of Joyce
Dennys near her home in Budleigh Salterton (p.165). Images from this trip were
included (uncredited) in the 1934 Shell Guide Cornwall Illustrated, edited by
Betjeman. In that year, Hoppé also took his picture of veteran zookeeper Ernie
Bowman feeding the German-born hippo, Joan (distinguished by the pink
markings on her legs), that had been acquired from Cologne for London Zoo
(p.154). At the end of 1935, Hoppé photographed the Sadler's Wells Ballet, taking
individual portraits of the sixteen-year-old Margot Fonteyn at the start of her
illustrious career (frontispiece, 56).

Much of Hoppé's late photojournalism in London formed the basis of his
1936 book Camera on Unknown London. This publication included his story on
Charles Burchett's tattoo parlour on Waterloo Road and Mr Guy Rouilly of Adam,

The Cab Drivers' Fare, Piccadilly, London, 1934, one of the studies for Hoppé's book *A Camera on Unknown London*, published 1936.

Rouilly & Co.'s shop at 18 Fitzroy Street, which imported and sold skeletons (pp.151–2). Other stories featured a group of cabmen in their shelter enjoying a cup of tea (above) and the nightwatchman at Ely Place, near Holborn Circus, still preserving the tradition of calling out every night 'Twelve o'clock of a misty night, and all's well' (p.147). Some of Hoppé's last pre-war pictures included documentation of the celebrations leading up to the Coronation, such as flag-making at Whiteley's department store (p.129), the staff at Buckingham Palace (p.145) and a portrait sitting with the wife and children of the German ambassador in London, and close friend of Adolf Hitler, Joachim von Ribbentrop.

In 1937 Hoppé left Millais House and focused on using his archive of photographs as the basis for the Dorien Leigh photographic agency, which he managed from the third floor of Ludgate House at 107 Fleet Street. When the Second World War broke out he was in Poland collecting material for another book, at which point he returned to London to concentrate on the agency. Dorien Leigh served as an outlet not only for his own work, but also for that of other photographers, and it contributed pictures to three mass-market illustrated magazines begun by the émigré Stefan Lorant: *Weekly Illustrated* (launched July 1934), *Lilliput* (from July 1937) and *Picture Post* (launched October 1938).

He never reopened his portrait studio, but characteristically continued to explore new fields of activity. He continued writing on a wide range of subjects, which he illustrated with his own photographs, occasionally adopting the name James Carr. To the end of his life he retained a lively interest in new ideas in photography, and his ninetieth birthday exhibition, organised by Kodak in 1968, featured some of the abstract and nature photographs, which had become his main interest during his last years. He died on 9 December 1972.

Notes

1 Graham Howe, 'Hoppé, Emil Otto (1878–1972)', in *Oxford Dictionary of National Biography* (Oxford: Oxford University Press, 2004).

2 Hoppé's 1911 application for naturalisation states that he had been living in the United Kingdom for eight years. The National Archives, Kew, HO/144/1169/214766.

3 *The Photographic Journal*, Vol.XLIII, No.10, November 1903.

4 Many of the contacts Hoppé made at the RPS would become his early portrait subjects.

5 Hoppé's exhibited works were no.167 *Brunette* and no.24 *Memento Mori* (the latter of which was reproduced in *Illustrated London News*, 7 October 1905, supplement, p.iv.

6 *Marion et Cie* is first listed in the *London Post Office Directory* in 1911 at 47 Dorset Street, Portman Square as 'French corset makers'. Her business is later listed at 56 Maddox Street, Mayfair, as 'Court Dressmakers'.

7 *The Photographic Journal*, Vol.XLVI, (supplement) September 1906: 51st Annual Exhibition, T.he New Gallery, 121 Regent Street, London. Hoppé, E.O., 4 George Yard, Lombard Strreet, EC. no.41 *The Visitor*, no.172 *Portrait of Cecil Heywood Esq*, no.265 *Critic*, no.279 *Portrait of A.L. Coburn. The Photographic Journal*, Vol. XLVI, (supplement) September 1907, 52nd Annual Exhibition: The New Gallery, 121 Regent Street, London. Hoppé, E.O. 10 Margravine Gardens, Baron's Court: no.175 *An Auld Licht*.

8 Hoppé's narrative study *The Visitor* was awarded Silver Plaque in the Photographic News Fourth Quarterly Competition, 25 January 1907. He also received a certificate for a second photograph, *A Modern Dance*.

9 A.H. Blake, 'The Man and His Aims', in *The Photographic News*, 18 October 1907, p.272.

10 Quotation from handwritten notes by E.O. Hoppé held at the E.O. Hoppé Estate Collection CA0042.

11 A portrait by Furley Lewis of Hoppé was published in *Amateur Photographer*, 28 April 1908, p.421 and a joint study of Hoppé and his wife Marion was included in the 1909 Dresden exhibition. It is possible that this image was the one used on their early Christmas card.

12 E.O. Hoppé, 'Rudolf Dührkoop's Aims & Methods in Photography', in *The Photographic Journal*, Vol.XLIX, No.2, February 1909, pp.96–103; E.O. Hoppé, 'Dies bildmäßige Behandlung Londons' in Fritz Loescher, *Deutscher Camera Almanach: ein Jahrbuch für die Photographie unserer Zeit* (Berlin: Gustav Schmidt, 1910) pp.15–26.

13 V. Rocco, 'Pictorialism and Modernism at the Dresden Internationale Photographische Ausstellung', in *History of Photography*, November 2009, pp.383–402; *Offizieller Katalog der Internationalen Photographischen Ausstellung* (Dresden: Wilhem Baensch, 1909).

14 Images taken for purposes of surveillance or classification.

15 M.F. Harker, *The Linked Ring* (London: Heinemann, 1979).

16 H. Snowden Ward F.R.P.S. 'The Work of the Year' *Photograms of the Year 1909* (London: Dawburn & Ward Ltd, 1909), p.41.

17 Hoppé's relaxed portrait of the former Viceroy of India, Lord Curzon, was taken on 27 July 1909 and published in the 4 August issue of the magazine. It was reproduced showing the full presentation print of four layers, the photographic print mounted on a signed tissue set off on a black tint and then presented on a further card.

18 Dr J.M. Bulloch (1868–1938) was editor of the *Graphic* 1909–24, the key years of Hoppé's portrait-taking, and his commission to photograph Mussolini in Rome, coincided with another Hoppé commission from Sunbeam cars to produce the book *To Rome on a Sunbeam* whose plates from *Camera Studies by E.O.Hoppé* included the forest of Fontainebleau, Avignon, Cannes, Tuscany, Orvieto and the Villa Medici, Rome. This project laid the basis for Hoppé's travel photography books that consumed a major part of his photographic activities until the outbreak of the Second World War. Bruce Ingram (1877–1963) was appointed editor of the *Illustrated London News* at the age of twenty-two in 1900 and continued to edit it until 1963, as well as editing the *Sketch* from 1905 to 1946.

19 Portraits published in the *Graphic*: 4 March 1911, p.305; 20 May 1911, p.751; 21 January 1911, p.97; 6 May 1911, p.651.

20 G. Craig, 'Youth and the Theatre Exhibition', in the *Graphic*, 3 June 1922, p.692.

21 Choreographed by Ruth St Denis and Ted Shawn to music by Walter Meyrowitz. First performed 29 July 1916 at the Greek Theatre, University of California, Berkeley. Later incorporated as part of the Egyptian Ballet (1922).

22 Goupil Gallery catalogue, nos.40–58.

23 Sale 1039, *Livres Illustres Modernes, Manuscrits et Photographies*, Christie's, Paris, 11 December 2001. Lot 1: *Portrait de Nijnsky dans le Spectre de la Rose*. Price realised: €7,165 ($6,420).

24 A. Wilson, 'Housed in Art History', in *Art Quarterly*, Spring & Winter 1994, pp.23–5, 26–9.

25 E.O. Hoppé, *Hundred Thousand Exposures* (London: Focal Press, 1945), p.19.

26 Black-and-white photographs of Mestrovic's work are included in *Exhibition of the Works of Ivan Mestrovic* (London: Victoria and Albert Museum, Summer 1915).

27 Birth certificate, London borough of Fulham.

28 E.O. Hoppé and Richard King *The Book of Fair Women* (London: Jonathan Cape, 1922).

29 Willa Cather was published in *Vanity Fair*, October 1921, p.62.

30 *The Fisherman* was published in *Vanity Fair*, August 1935, p.35.

31 *The Bookman,* May 1914, pp.85–7.

32 *The Bookman,* December 1924, p.151.

33 *Fire under the Andes. A group of North American portraits*, text by Elizabeth Shepley Sergeant, photographs by Hoppé (New York: Knopf, 1927).

34 E.O. Hoppé and Richard King, 1922, op. cit.

35 *Bystander*, 12 February 1913, p.345.

36 *The New York Times,* 16 August 1920, p.10.

37 This was one of many charitable theatrical events that Hazel Martyn, the American-born second wife of the fashionable portraitist Sir John Lavery, helped organise during the First World War.

38 Lady Cynthia Asquith's diaries, 15 June 1916 quoted in S. McCoole, *Hazel: A Life of Lady Lavery* (Dublin: The Lilliput Press Ltd, 1996), p.60.

39 E.O. Hoppé, 1945, op.cit., p.90.

40 *The Times*, 1 June 1921, p.13.

41 *Colour*, issue 1, p.2.

42 E.O. Hoppé, 1945, op.cit., p.118.

43 In 1919, Hoppé designed sets for Basil Hood's *The Great Silence* with A.L. Coburn, and for Antonio Cippico's *The Night of the Three Kings*. The Plough 1919 manifesto (printed in London by Herbert Reach), p.3.

44 *New Camera Work by E.O. Hoppé* (London: The Goupil Gallery, January 1922).

45 *New Camera Work by E.O. Hoppé*, (London: Millais House, 1922), back cover.

46 Dita Parlo's career has recently been rediscovered by a modern audience after Madonna used her persona as an alter-ego in her notorious photo-book *Sex* and album *Erotica* in 1992, and more recently, after the American-born burlesque dancer Heather Sweet re-invented herself as Dita von Teese.

47 *Daily Mirror,* 15 August 1908, p.11.

48 *Graphic*, 16 April 1932, pp.569–71.

49 Ibid., 19 April 1930, p.123.

50 Ibid., 12 March 1932, pp.392–4.

51 Hoppé also took photographs in spring 1931 at the Natural History Museum and at the Victoria and Albert Museum, including some cleaners dusting the exhibits. (Hoppé negative register number 19678).

52 *Illustrated London News*, Saturday, 23 September 1933; p.461, Issue 4927.

53 *Münchner Illustrierte Preße*, 30 April 1928. *Berliner Illustrirte Zeitung*, No.26, 26 June 1927 (frontispiece).

54 *Weekly Illustrated* was founded in July 1934 by Stefan Lorant who had fled Nazi Germany and worked with a team of outstanding émigré photographers such as Hans Baumann (Felix H. Man) and Kurt Hübschmann (Hutton), and British photographers Humphrey Spender and Bill Brandt. Lorant was instrumental in launching *Picture Post* in 1938, to which the same photographers contributed.

FAIR WOMEN

More than any other publication, *The Book of Fair Women* established Hoppé as a connoisseur of female beauty. Published in 1922, the collection of thirty-two portraits of women eschewed accepted Western notions of beauty in featuring representatives from around the world and from a variety of racial groups. Hoppé maintained that true beauty came from freedom and intellectual fulfilment. His assertion that women from other cultures could be as beautiful as the Europeans was met by a furore in the international press, and the effect that the publication had on his career as an arbiter of feminine beauty far exceeded the number of copies of the book that were sold.

Dutch West Indies, 1921
Hebe (Constance Vessellier), 1917

Lady Lavery, 1916
Viscountess Massereene and Ferrard, 1916
Haitian Beauty, 1921

Cuban Beauty, 1921
Princess White Deer, 1921
Lady Diana Cooper, 1916

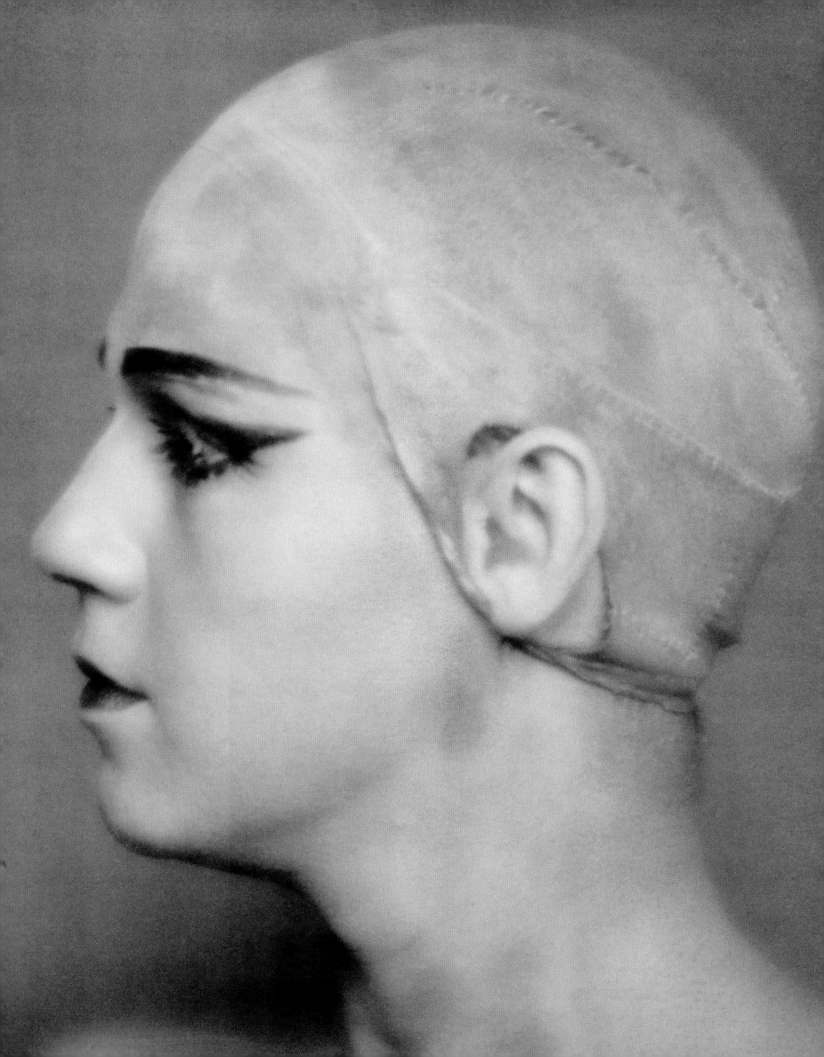

STUDIO

_____

Ted Shawn in *Tillers of the Soil*, 1922

Olga Spessivtseva as Aurora in *The Sleeping Princess*, 1921

Vaslav Nijinsky as Spectre de la Rose in *Le Spectre de la Rose,* 1914

Léon Bakst, 1913

Tamara Karsavina, 1912

Vaslav Nijinsky as Spectre de la Rose in *Le Spectre de la Rose,* 1914

Tamara Karsavina and Adolph Bolm in *Thamar*, 1912

Tamara Karsavina as Columbine in *Carnaval*, 1912

Vera Fokina as Zobeida and Michel Fokine as the Favourite Slave in *Scheherazade*, 1914

Martha Graham and Ted Shawn, 1922

Clotilde von Derp (Madame Sakharoff), 1911

Margot Fonteyn, 1935

Beatrice Appleyard, 1934

Hermione Darnborough, 1934

Tilly Losch, 1928

Max Reinhardt, 1911

Paul Robeson, 1926

Edward Gordon Craig, 1911

Ellen Terry as the Nurse in *Romeo and Juliet,* 1919

Elizabeth Nelvi Craig, 1913

Elizabeth Nelvi Craig, 1924

Gina Palerme, 1915

Gina Palerme in costume for *Bric-à-Brac*
at the Palace Theatre, 1915

Marion Davies, 1921

Lillian Gish, 1921

Brigitte Helm, 1928

Fritz Lang, 1929

Mimi Jordan, 1925

Anna May Wong, 1926

Teddie Gerrard, 1915

Sylvia Gough, 1916

Biddy Willoughby, 1931

Eileen Hawthorne, 1931

Filippo Tommaso Marinetti, 1912

Lady Lavery as William-Adolphe
Bouguereau's *Vierge Consolatrice*
with Violet de Trafford, 1916

William Nicholson, 1912

Jacob Epstein in front of his
memorial for Oscar Wilde, 1912

Marsden Hartley, 1923

Paul Manship with a cast of *The Spear Thrower,* 1921

Käthe Kollwitz, 1927

Nicholas Roerich, 1920

Samuel Coleridge-Taylor, 1912

William Strang, 1909

Gluck, 1924

Alan Odle, 1915

Rabindranath Tagore, 1920

Ezra Pound, 1918

Rudyard Kipling, 1912

Thomas Hardy, 1914

Sir Arthur Conan Doyle, 1912

Peter Llewellyn Davies, 1916

W. Somerset Maugham, 1912

Vita Sackville-West, 1916

Henry James, 1911

Rebecca West, 1923

John Masefield, 1912

Violet Hunt, 1912

Anita Loos, 1926

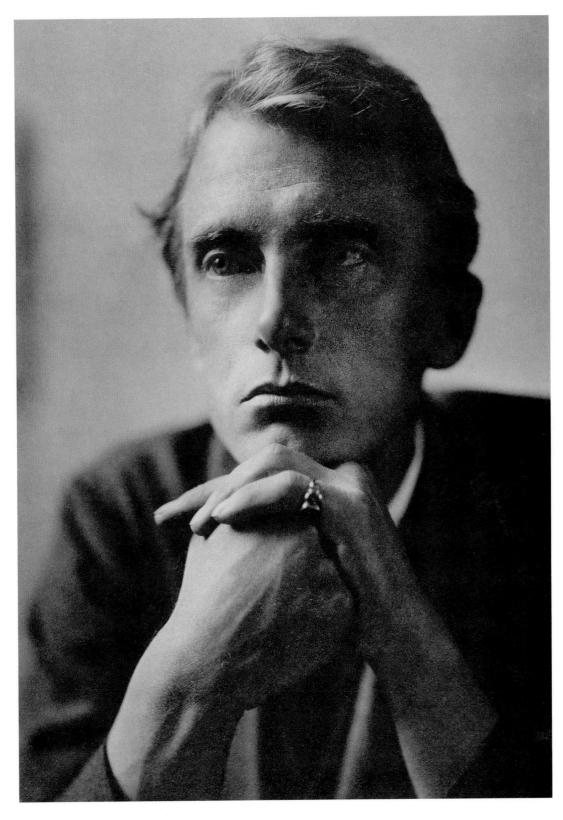

Edward Thomas, 1911

Havelock Ellis, 1922

Marguerite Salle, 1934

Albert Einstein, 1921

King George V, 1921

Elizabeth Bowes-Lyon, Duchess of York, later
Queen Elizabeth, the Queen Mother, 1923

The Duke and Duchess of York, later King George VI
and Queen Elizabeth, the Queen Mother, 1923

David Lloyd George, 1911

Benito Mussolini, 1924

Big Chief White Horse Eagle of the Osagi tribe, Oklahoma, 1926

Maori Chief, New Zealand, 1929

George Bernard Shaw at his home,
10 Adelphi Terrace, London, 1923

George Bernard Shaw on the balcony of
his home, 10 Adelphi Terrace, London, 1923

TYPES

Hoppé's fascination with personality and type culminated in the publication of two books: *Taken from Life* in 1922 and *London Types* in 1926. The portraits included in these titles reflect his enduring interest in social types, recording the characteristics he saw as typical among people he met on his excursions through London and the rest of the world. While these portraits share some of the stylistic conventions of Hoppé's studio work, they were usually cropped to head or busts only. Hoppé's intention was to present these types not as individuals, but as representative of particular groups of people that he saw vanishing from society.

Flower Seller, London, 1921
Home Workers, London, 1921
Prime of Life, London, c.1921
Mrs Bennett, 1921

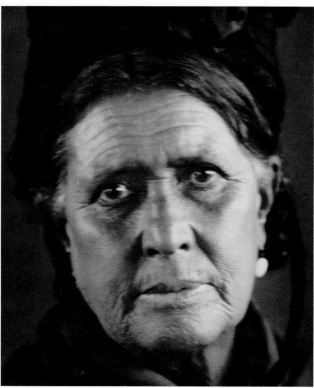

New York, 1921
Vedic Scholar, Gwalior, 1929
Flora, Flower Lady, Piccadilly Circus, London, 1921
Young Brahmin Woman, Guntakal, 1929

A Sinhalese Gentleman, 1929
Highly Respectable, London, c.1912
New York, 1921
Postman, 1913

THE
BEST FURNITURE
comes from
The Times FURNISHING Co. Ltd.
$1 a month buys $40 worth
... CHES AT
... HAM RD. BRIXTON
... HALL CROYDON

STREET

―――

British Museum Underground Station, London, 1937

Speakers' Corner, Hyde Park, London, 1934

Bank Holiday in the Park, London, 1929
Sketching, Hyde Park, London, 1934
Policeman overlooking swimmers and
sunbathers at Serpentine Lido, Hyde Park,
London, 1935

Sandhurst Royal Military College, Surrey, 1932

Physical education, The King's School, Canterbury, Kent, 1939

New recruits at Central London Army Recruiting Depot, 1932

Sandhurst Royal Military College, Surrey, 1932

Street musicians, London, 1945

Flag-making for the Coronation at Whiteley's, London, 1937

Children, Limehouse, London, 1932

The Pearlies, Master William Dennis Simmons, London, 1922

Ras Prince Monolulu, London, 1929

'Buffalo Bill' from Bengal, East End type, London, 1933

Sandwich board man advertising Shafi Hindustan
Restaurant, 18 Gerrard Street, London, 1945

Refreshment rooms, West India Dock Road, London, 1934

At the counter in a snack bar, London, 1935

At the counter in a snack bar, London, 1935

Passengers on a bus, London, 1945

Drinking tea in the busmans' canteen, London, 1936

Westminster Underground Station, London, 1937

Exiting Tottenham Court Road Underground Station, London, 1937

Savoy Hotel waiters feeding birds, London, 1937

Regent Street, London, 1934

Waitress, Miss Vyse, the original 'Nippy', London, 1924

Thomas Williams, Superintendant of Buckingham Palace, London, 1937

Nightwatchman, Bank of England, London, 1925

Nightwatchman, Ely Place, London, 1935

Deskwork at the British Union of Fascists,
Black House, King's Road, Chelsea, London, 1934

Sleeping on the street, Trafalgar Square, London, 1935

Artists of the Hagenbeck Circus, London, 1935

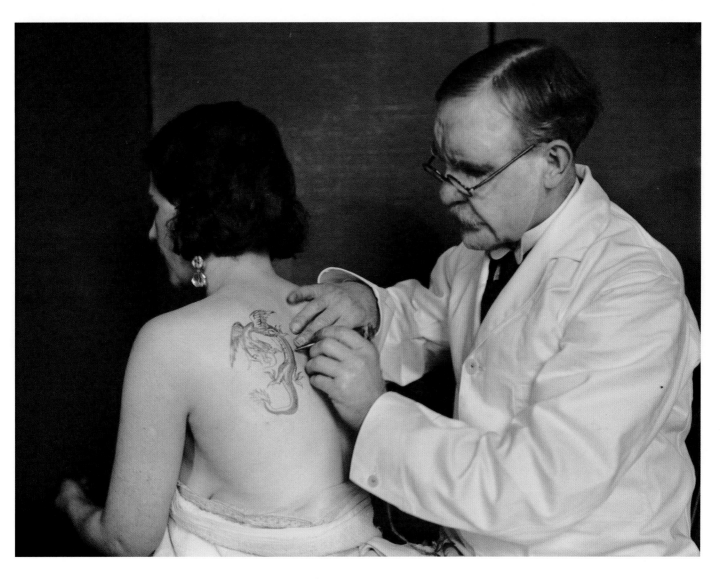

Charles Burchett tattooing a woman's back, Waterloo Road, London, 1931

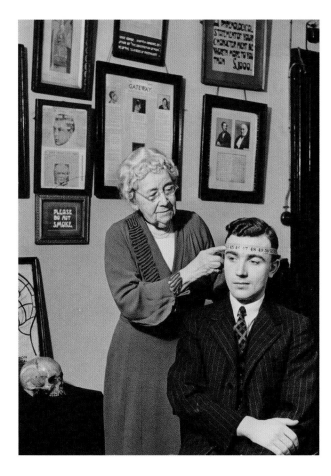

Phrenologist, Catherine Stackpool O'Dell, London, 1936

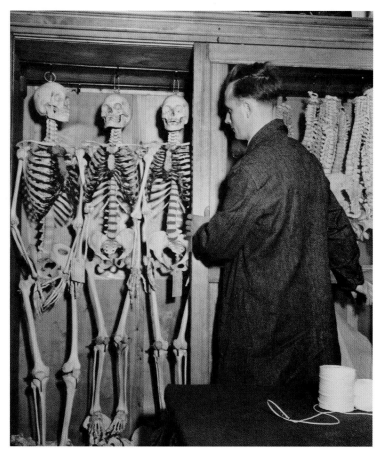

Guy Rouilly, Adam Rouilly & Co., Skeleton Shop, London, 1935

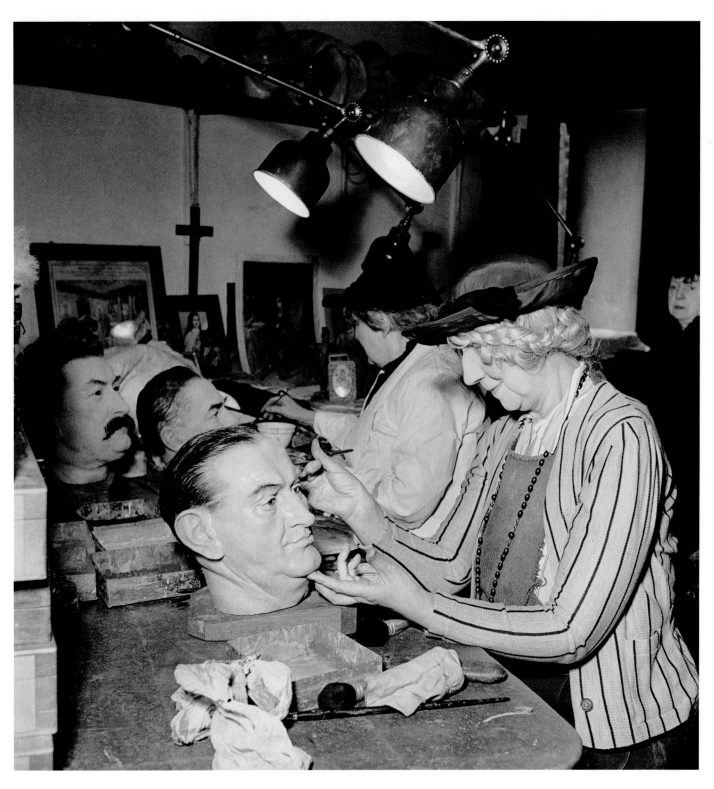

Making waxworks at Madame Tussaud's, London, 1935

Zookeeper, Ernie Bowman and hippopotamus, Joan, London, 1934

Naturalist mounting a stuffed bird, London, 1930s

Dog Cemetery, Hyde Park, London, 1933

In the waiting room at the dog hospital, Croydon, 1935

Bell Ringers at St Olave's Church, Hart Street, London, 1935

The Organ of the Royal Albert Hall, London, 1935

Girls at swimming pool, Borstal Institute, Aylesbury, Buckinghamshire, 1937

Girls dancing to gramophone, Borstal Institute, Aylesbury, Buckinghamshire, 1937

Percussion band, Roedean school, Brighton, Sussex, 1935
Organist at Old Mill Church, Reigate, Surrey, 1937

Student ironing in the pantry, Lady Margaret Hall, Oxford, 1935
Children's Christmas Party, London, 1932

Felling trees at Rag, Galhampton, Somerset, 1940s

Joyce Dennys, Budleigh Salterton, Devon, 1932

CHRONOLOGY

1878
Sunday, 14 April: Emil Otto born to
Marie and Philipp Hoppé in Munich.

1902
Moves to London, where he works
in the Deutsche Bank and takes up
photography as a hobby.

1903
Elected as a member of the Royal
Photographic Society (RPS).

1905
Two works are selected for exhibition
at the RPS Salon, (*Memento Mori* and
Brunette). Marries Marion Josephine
Wilhelmina Bliersbach at Fulham
Registry Office, London.

1906–7
Regular prizewinner and exhibitor
at photographic exhibitions and
awarded a Fellowship of the Royal
Photographic Society (FRPS).

1907
October: Hoppé opens his first
studio, at 10 Margravine Gardens,
near Barons Court, London.

1908
15 August: Hoppé's first press
photograph, taken at the Franco-
British Exhibition, White City, London,
is published in the *Daily Mirror*.

1909
With Sir Benjamin Stone, Hoppé
represents Great Britain at
the *International Exhibition of
Photography* at Dresden, Germany.

1909–10
Co-founder of the London Salon of
Photography, which succeeded the
Linked Ring Salon. Hoppé exhibits
four subject pictures and a portrait
of Sara De Groote.

1910
April–May: first one-man show, of
seventy-two photographs, at Royal
Photographic Society, RPS House,
55 Russell Square, London.

Tableau of Lute-Playing and Singing Angels, 1917,
after *The Nativity*, 1490–5, by Piero della Francesca.
From *Tableaux of Angels: After the Great Masters*,
published in aid of the British Women's Hospital
Appeal in Aid of the Nation's Fund for Nurses.

1911
Moves to larger studio at 59 Baker Street. Photographs leading members of Diaghilev's Russian Ballet.

1912
Hoppé naturalised as a British citizen. 18 January: first child, Frank Sidney Hoppé, born.

1913
February: one-man exhibition at the Goupil Gallery.
Moves his studio to 7 Cromwell Place, South Kensington, London, and renames it Millais House.

1914
New art magazine, *Colour*, launched. Hoppé is art editor and contributes reviews, designs and drawings.
14 December: second child, Muriel Marion Hoppé, born.

1916
September: British *Vogue* launched. Hoppé contributes editorial and society photographs to early issues.

1917
Founder and committee member of The Plough theatre club. Members include architect Charles Rennie Mackintosh, who designs the extension for the Hoppé family home at Little Hedgecourt, Sussex (below).

1920
16 August: the *New York Times* announces the arrival of Hoppé in the USA on the *Caronia* in search of beauties for the proposed *Book of Fair Women*.

E.O. Hoppé and family at Little Hedgecourt, East Grinstead, Sussex by A.L. Coburn, *c.*1920

1921
Takes portrait sittings in his New York studio on 57th Street, including film stars Anna Q. Nilsson, Lillian Gish, Mary Miles Minter, Marion Davies, and artists Paul Manship and James Montgomery Flagg. Holds first major US exhibition at the Wanamaker Gallery, New York.
December: invited to Buckingham Palace to photograph George V.

1922
January: major one-man show, of 221 exhibits, at the Goupil Gallery (catalogue introduction by John Galsworthy).
June–July: *International Theatre Exhibition* at Victoria and Albert Museum. Hoppé is on the organising committee and contributes stage and costume designs.

1923
Visits Romania, as guest of Queen Marie and the Romanian royal family, to collect material for his first travel book, *In Gipsy Camp and Royal Palace*. *Photographic Masterpieces by E.O. Hoppé*, staged by the Asahi Shimbun Company of Tokyo in Ueno, Japan.

1924
Travels to Italy; photographs Mussolini in Rome for the *Graphic*. Commissioned by J. Lyons & Co. to photograph the first 'Nippy' waitress.

1925
Travels around Britain and Ireland photographing topography for his first book in the Orbis Terrarum series.

1926
Returns to America, takes portraits in New York, visits Hollywood. Spends time with Native American tribes. Visits Cuba, Jamaica and West Indies.

RUMANIAN GYPSY

Rumanian Gypsy, c.1923. Published in Konrad Bercovici's book, *The Story of the Gypsies* (1929) along with seven other plates by E.O. Hoppé. The images were most likely taken during his travels to Romania in the summer of 1923.

Mrs Brandt, 1927. Published to accompany the chapter 'Skyscrapers and Women' in *Unterwegs* (En Route) (1931).

1927
May: exhibition of *Rural England* photographs at Dover Gallery, London, to mark publication of *Picturesque Great Britain*. Takes portrait sittings in Berlin and photographs for the Ufa Film Studios; undertakes topographical and industrial photography.

1929
Travels to India, Ceylon (Sri Lanka), Australia and New Zealand.

1930
Exhibition *79 Camera Pictures* held at David Jones' Department Store, Sydney, Australia.

1935
Launch of *Geographical Magazine* to which Hoppé becomes contributor and art editor.

1931–9
Travels to Indonesia, Bali, Africa, Bavaria, Poland and Czechoslovakia.

1937
Leaves Millais House, which is taken over as studio by ballet photographer Gordon Anthony, and subsequently artist Francis Bacon.

1939
Returns to London at outbreak of war. Concentrates on Dorien Leigh photographic agency.

1954
Exhibition *A Half Century of Photography* at Foyles Art Gallery, London, opened by James Laver (exhibition later held at Lenbachhaus, Munich, and then toured by British Council in India and Far East).

1968
Photographed and interviewed by John Hedgecoe for *Queen* magazine and exhibition at Kodak Gallery to mark Hoppé's ninetieth birthday.

1972
Receives Royal Photographic Society Honorary Fellowship.
Dies on 9 December, aged ninety-four.

E.O. Hoppé by
Cecil Beaton, January 1969

E.O. HOPPÉ'S PUBLICATIONS

E.O. Hoppé and Auguste Bert, *Studies from the Russian Ballet* (London: Fine Art Society, 1913)

Sir Claude Phillips, annotations on the original pictures with fifteen camera studies by E.O. Hoppé, *Tableaux of Angels: After the Great Masters* (Published in aid of the British Women's Hospital Appeal in aid of the Nation's Fund for Nurses, 1917)

John Davys Beresford, with seven photogravure plates by E.O. Hoppé, *Taken From Life* (London: Collins, 1922)

E.O. Hoppé and Minya Diez-Dührkoop, *Die schöne Frauen* (Munich: Bruckmann, 1922)

E.O. Hoppé and Richard King, *The Book of Fair Women* (New York: Knopf; London: Jonathan Cape; Munich: Bruckmann, 1922)

Joseph Thorp, with ten studies by E.O. Hoppé, *Behind the Machine* (London: Oriel Press, 1922)

Arthur St John Adcock, with thirty-two portraits by E.O. Hoppé, *Gods of Modern Grub Street: Impressions of Contemporary Authors* (London: Sampson Low, Marston and Co., 1923)

E.O. Hoppé, preface by the Queen of Rumania, *In Gipsy Camp and Royal Palace: Wanderings in Rumania* (London: Methuen, 1924; New York: Scribners, 1924)

To Rome on a Sunbeam (Wolverhampton: Sunbeam Motor Car Company, 1924)

E.O. Hoppé, *A Collection of Photographic Masterpieces by E.O. Hoppé* (Tokyo: Asahi Shimbun, 1925)

Tancred Borenius, with special photographs by E.O. Hoppé, *Forty London Statues and Public Monuments* (London: Methuen, 1926)

Peter Landow, 120 plates with fifteen by E.O. Hoppé, *Nature and Culture: Woman* (London: Chapman & Hall, 1926)

W. Pett Ridge, with portraits by E.O. Hoppé, *London Types: Taken from Life* (London: Methuen, 1926)

E.O. Hoppé, with an introduction by Charles F.G. Masterman, *Picturesque Great Britain: The Architecture and the Landscape* (Orbis Terrarum series: New York: Brentano's, 1926; Berlin: Ernst Wasmuth, 1926; London: Benn, 1927)/*L'Angleterre: architecture et paysages* (Paris: Librairie des arts décoratifs, c.1927)

E.O. Hoppé, *Romantic America: Picturesque United States* (New York: Westermann, 1927)/*Das Romantische Amerika* (Berlin: Ernst Wasmuth, 1927)/*Les États-Unis d'Amérique: architecture et paysages* (Paris: Librairie des arts décoratifs, c.1927)

Elizabeth Shepley Sergeant, with photographs by E.O. Hoppé, *Fire under the Andes: A Group of North American Portraits* (New York: Knopf, 1927)

Arthur St John Adcock, with thirty-two portraits by E.O. Hoppé, *The Glory that Was Grub Street: Impressions of Contemporary Authors* (London: Sampson, Low, Marston, 1928)

Hermann and Marianne Aubel, with three plates by E.O. Hoppé, *Der künstlerische Tanz unserer Zeit* (Taunus and Leipzig: Königstein, 1928)

Konrad Bercovici, with eight plates by E.O. Hoppé, *The Story of the Gipsies* (London: Cape, 1929)

E.O. Hoppé, with an introduction by Bruno H. Burgel, *Deutsche Arbeit* (Berlin: Ullstein, 1930)

E.O. Hoppé, *The Fifth Continent* (London: Simpkin Marshall, 1931)/*Der fünfte Kontinent* (Berlin: Atlantis, 1931)

Tänze von Anna Pawlowa im Bilde, with thirty-two plates, ten by E.O. Hoppé (including cover) (Dresden: Carl Reissner, 1931)

E.O. Hoppé, *Romantik der Kleinstadt* (Munich: Bruckmann, 1932)

E.O. Hoppé, *Unterwegs* (Berlin: Ernst Pollak, 1932)

E.O. Hoppé, *London* (London: Medici Society Picture Guide Series, 1932)/*Londres* (Grenoble: Arthaud, 1933)

Daniel Masclet, *La Beauté de la femme: album du premier salon international du nu photographique, Paris 1933* (Paris: Daniel Masclet, 1933)

A.G. Street, with eight photographs by E.O.Hoppé, *Country Days* (London: Faber and Faber, 1933)

John Betjeman (ed.), *Cornwall Illustrated, In a Series of Views* (London: Architectural Press, 1934)

E.O. Hoppé, *Round the World with a Camera* (London: Hutchinson, 1934)

E.O. Hoppé, *The Image of London: A Hundred Photographs* (London: Chatto & Windus, 1935)

Katherine Mayo, *The Face of Mother India*, (London: Hamish Hamilton, 1935)

E.O. Hoppé, *A Camera on Unknown London: Sixty Photographs and Descriptive Notes of Curiosities of London to be Seen Today* (London: Dent, 1936)

Nudes of All Nations: 48 Photographic Studies (London: Routledge, 1936)

E.O. Hoppé, *The London of George VI* (London: Dent, 1937)

Ceylon by Orient Line (London: Orient Line, c.1937)

E.O. Hoppé, with an introduction by Cecil Beaton, *Hundred Thousand Exposures: The Success of a Photographer* (London and New York: Focal Press, 1945)

World's People and How They Live (London: Odhams, 1946)

E.O. Hoppé, *Rural London in Pictures* (London: Odhams, 1951)

E.O. Hoppé, with Karl-Heinz Jaeckel, *Blaue Berge von Jamaica* (Berlin: Safari, 1956)

E.O. Hoppé, *Pirates, Buccaneers and Gentlemen Adventurers* (New York: Barnes and London: Yoseloff, 1972)

FURTHER READING

Michel Auer, *Encyclopédie internationale des photographes de 1839* (Hermance, Switzerland: Editions Camera Obscura, 1985)

Cecil Beaton, *British Photographers* (London: Collins, 1944)

Cecil Beaton and Gail Buckland, *The Magic Image: The Genius of Photography from 1839 to the Present Day* (London: Weidenfeld and Nicolson, 1975)

Diana P. Daniels, 'One Man's View: E.O. Hoppé and the Diaghilev Ballet', *Dance Magazine*, September 1954, pp.16–20

Dictionary of National Biography (Oxford: Oxford University Press, 1993)

William A. Ewing, *The Fugitive Gesture: Masterpieces of Dance Photography* (London: Thames and Hudson, 1987)

Helmut Gernsheim (ed.) with a foreword by Rathbone Holme, *The Man Behind the Camera* (London: Fountain Press, 1948)

Helmut Gernsheim with Alison Gernsheim, *The History of Photography: From the Earliest Use of the Camera Obscura in the Eleventh Century Up to 1914* (London: Oxford University Press, 1955)

Helmut Gernsheim, *Creative Photography: Aesthetic Trends 1839–1960* (New York: Bonanza Books, 1962)

Mark Haworth-Booth, *Hoppé's London* (London: Guiding Light, 2006)

John Hedgecoe, 'Hello, Mr Hoppé' in *Queen*, 3 July 1968, pp.50–3

Graham Howe, 'Hoppé, Emil Otto (1878–1972)', *Oxford Dictionary of National Biography* (Oxford: Oxford University Press, 2004)

Graham Howe and Erika Esau, *E.O. Hoppé's Australia* (New York: Norton, 2007)

Robin Lenman (ed.), *The Oxford Companion to the Photograph* (Oxford: Oxford University Press, 2005)

Eric de Maré, *Photography* (Harmondsworth: Penguin, 1957)

Ruth Matthews, *Who's Who in Photography* (London: Focal Press, 1951)

David Mellor, 'Patterns of Naturalism: Hoppé to Hardy' in *The Real Thing: An Anthology of British Photography* (London: Arts Council, 1975), pp.25–35

Colin Naylor (ed.), *Contemporary Photographers* (Chicago and London: St. James, 1988)

Philip Prodger, *E.O. Hoppé's Amerika: Modernist Photographs from the 1920s* (New York: Norton, 2007)

Naomi Rosenblum, *A World History of Photography* (New York: Abbeville Press, 1984)

Brian Stokoe, 'The Image of London: The Metropolitan Photography of E.O. Hoppé' *London Journal*, vol.2, no. 30, 2005, pp.40–65

Brian Stokoe, 'Class Tourism and Photography: The Typological Portraits of E.O. Hoppé and J.D. Beresford' in *History of Photography*, vol.31, no.2, Summer 2007, pp.180–200

Studies in Visual Communication, vol.11, Spring 1985

Jane Turner (ed.), *The Dictionary of Art* (London: Macmillan, 1996)

Who's Who 1928 (London; A&C Black Limited, 1927) pp.1467–8 and entries until 1972

Val Williams and Terence Pepper (eds), with an essay by Ian Jeffrey, *Cities and Industry: Camera Pictures by E.O. Hoppé* (York: Impressions Gallery, 1978)

Lee D. Witkin and Barbara London, *The Photograph Collector's Guide* (London: Secker and Warburg, 1979)

ACKNOWLEDGEMENTS

Towards the end of his life, E.O. Hoppé expressed frustration that the universal acclaim he once enjoyed had faded. He never lived to see a retrospective such as this book represents, and it was only after the personal intercession of the late art historian Bill Jay that he was accorded an Honorary Fellowship by the Royal Photographic Society in 1972, just a month or so before he died. This pleased Hoppé enormously, and Jay deserves enormous credit for his advocacy and foresight. Recognition mattered a great deal to Hoppé, and if he were still among us, he would have wholeheartedly thanked each and every one of the marvellous staff at the National Portrait Gallery and the E.O. Hoppé Estate Collection for making possible this handsome publication and the accompanying exhibition.

I am deeply indebted to colleagues at the National Portrait Gallery for welcoming me as Guest Curator of this exhibition, and am particularly thankful to Curator of Photographs Terence Pepper for graciously inviting me to work on a project with which he has such a distinguished history. His pioneering exhibition of 1978, *Camera Portraits by E.O. Hoppé,* together with subsequent publications and acquisitions at the Gallery render him the unquestioned authority in the field, and were it not for his punishing schedule he would, by rights, have organised the exhibition himself.

I am grateful to Sandy Nairne, Director of the National Portrait Gallery, for his enthusiastic support. His insight and powerful vision for programmes at the Gallery are apparent to all who have the pleasure to work with him. Sarah Tinsley, Head of Exhibitions and Collections Management, spearheaded the project seemingly effortlessly. Exhibitions Manager Sophie Clark was given the unenviable task of coordinating the project either side of the Atlantic and was tireless in her expert assistance. I am also grateful to Inga Fraser, Flora Fricker, Eleanor Macnair, Ulrike Wachsmann, and the registration, design, and installation teams at the Gallery for their contributions. Special thanks also go to Editor Claudia Bloch for her meticulous work improving the manuscript, and for skilfully synthesising a compelling whole from occasionally disparate parts. Claudia Sorsby, who has yet to find a text she couldn't improve, provided helpful comments on early drafts of the manuscript. Special thanks too, to Dan Monroe, Lynda Hartigan, and the staff at the Peabody Essex Museum, Salem, Massachusetts for enabling me to join this project, and especially to April Swieconek for her help with various aspects in the United States.

It has been my great privilege to work on this and related projects with Graham Howe, Director of the E.O. Hoppé Estate Collection. I am enormously grateful for his confidence and trust, and thank him for making the full resources of the Hoppé picture and manuscript collections available to me. I am also grateful for the work of his associates in Pasadena: Jeremy Bigalke, Elena Kordik, Sam Mellon, Aaron Owsiany and, early in the project, Pam Moffat. It is no exaggeration to say that the collection would not exist as it does had it not been for Graham's determined campaign to remove it intact from the Mansell Collection, where it had been split up and largely lost to scholarship. It took an extraordinary man to sink all his resources into restoring the legacy of an artist with whom he had no personal connection, but in whom he believes passionately.

Phillip Prodger

I first came across E.O. Hoppé's life and work in 1974 when my first job after university and a librarianship qualification took me to the Mansell Collection, a historical picture library in Notting Hill Gate that had acquired his archive and picture library in the 1950s. I was immediately struck by the quality of the work and, out of hours, started compiling a checklist of surviving portrait prints and, with the help of fellow research assistant Ursula McMullan, transcribing the 15,000 or so sittings recorded in his sitters books between the years 1908 and 1934. A year later I joined the National Portrait Gallery, under Director John Hayes and Keeper of Film and Photography, Colin Ford, who agreed it would be appropriate that we should hold a centenary exhibition of Hoppé's portrait photographs in 1978. I was greatly encouraged by my previous employers, the Directors of the Mansell Collection, Miss Louie Boutroy and George Anderson, as well as Hoppé's son, Frank Hoppé, who held a further archive of work, and surviving sitters, such as Lady Diana Cooper, Rebecca West and most particularly the painter Gluck.

In the 1990s Graham Howe, a long-standing enthusiast for Hoppé's work, was able to acquire the collection and moved it to its current housing at Curatorial Assistance in Pasadena. After a long period of conservation, cataloguing and digitisation, an exciting exhibition, set out with the vision of photo-historian Phillip Prodger, was proposed. It was decided that the Gallery should stage a second show that would also focus on Hoppé's lesser known reportage and photojournalism of the 1930s.

I am most grateful to my Director, Sandy Nairne, for being able to review and update my original research from the 1978 show, my colleagues in the Photographs Department at the National Portrait Gallery and others thanked elsewhere in this publication especially, Exhibitions Manager Sophie Clark. Researching this new collection of work would not have been possible without the help of Inga Fraser, who has helped make many fascinating discoveries with a meticulous care for accuracy and constant and inspirational thoroughness. We are grateful to the following for sharing information in their archives and their own specialist knowledge. They include: H.J.P. Arnold (biographer of Herbert Ponting), Janet Austin (local historian in West Sussex), Rita Bosworth (Consultant Archivist, Westminster School), Nicola Byrne (Ellen Terry Museum, Smallhythe Place), Patrick Collins (National Motor Museum Trust), Christine Comer (Croydon Local Studies Library and Archive), Allison Derrett (Assistant Registrar, Royal Archives), Dr Tim Eggington (Whipple Librarian, University of Cambridge), Peter Grove (Food Historian), Jennifer Gyr, Peter Henderson (Archivist at The King's School, Canterbury), Noneen Jacques, Ruth Kitchin (Curator of Collections Access, National Media Museum, Bradford), Sinead McCoole (Biographer of Hazel Lavery), Emma Milnes (Retrospective Book Cataloguer, London Zoo), Oliver Mahony (Archivist, Lady Margaret Hall), Mark Morre (PDX History), Andrew Orgill (Senior Librarian, Royal Military Academy, Sandhurst), Norton Owen (Director of Preservation, Jacob's Pillow Dance Festival), Jane Pritchard (Curator of Dance, Victoria and Albert Museum), Helen Speake (Dogs Trust), John Smith (Finsbury Library, London Borough of Islington), Jackie Sullivan (Archivist, Roedean school).

Finally, I should like to thank my Editor, Claudia Bloch who managed to help properly order all our research and travelled with me to California and see the works at first hand at Curatorial Assistance. For additional travel and research costs we are very grateful for two grants from the EP Trust.

Terence Pepper

INDEX

Unless otherwise stated, all page references in *italics* are to works by E.O. Hoppé.

A
Abbe, James 36
Adam, Rouilly & Co. 37–8
Adcock, Arthur St John 32
Alexandra, Queen 34
Appleyard, Beatrice *57*
Arbuthnot, Malcolm 28, 30
Armfield, Maxwell 34
Artists of the Hagenbeck Circus 150
Asahi Shimbun Company 35, 168
Auld Licht, An 27
Aumonier, Stacy, *Odd Fish: Being a Casual Selection of London Residents Described and Drawn* 19

B
Bakst, Léon 30, *48*
Ballets Russes 13, 30
Bank Holiday in the Park 123
Barrett, Alfred Wilson 34
Bartels, Hans von 26, 30
Bassano, Alexander, *England's Beautiful Women* 33
Bauhaus 13
Bax, Clifford and Arnold 35
Beaton, Cecil 13, 14, 30
    Book of Beauty, The 33
    E.O. Hoppé (portrait) *169*
Belcher, George 19, 36
Bell Ringers at St Olave's Church, Hart Street 158
Bennett, Arnold 30, *31*, 32
Beresford, G.C. 26
Beresford, J.D. 19
Bert, Auguste 30
Betjeman, John 37
Bloomsbury Group 13
Bolm, Adolph 30, *51*
Bouguereau, William-Adolphe, *Vierge Consolatrice* 33
Bowman, Ernie 37, *154*
Brangwyn, Frank 29
British Museum Underground Station 120
Budleigh Salterton 37
'Buffalo Bill' from Bengal 133
Bulloch, Dr J.M. 29, 35
Burchett, Charles 37, *151*

C
Cab Drivers' Fare, Piccadilly, The 38, *38*
cameras
    bellows-type 14
    miniature 16
    twin-lens reflex 14
Camera Work 28
Cameron, Julia Margaret 12, 31
Carbro Colour 14
Carroll, Lewis 31
Caruso, Enrico 29
Cather, Willa 32
Cecil, Hugh 28
    Book of Beauty, A 33
Charlady (1920s) *18*, *19*
Charles Burchett tattooing a woman's back, Waterloo Road 151
chiaroscuro 12, 18
Children, Limehouse 130
Children's Christmas Party 163
Clausen, George 35
Clemenceau, Georges 10, *10*, 11
Coburn, Alvin Langdon 26, 27, 28, 35
    E. O. Hoppé and family 167
Coleridge-Taylor, Samuel *86*
Colour 34–5
Conan Doyle, Sir Arthur 11, *94*
Concerts at the Front Fund 33
Cookesley, Margaret 31
Cooper, Lady Diana (née Manners) 33, 34, *43*
Cooper, Gladys 34, *34*
Cornuel, Madame 10
Cornwall Illustrated 37
Coronation (1937) 33, 38, *129*
Craig, Edward Gordon 11, 30, 34, *62*
Craig, Elizabeth Nelvi *64*, *65*
Critic, The 27
Cuban Beauty 43
Cunard, Nancy 33
Curzon, George Nathaniel, Marquess 28

D
Daily Mirror 36
Darnborough, Hermione *58*
Davies, Marion 33, 34, *68*
Decorative Arts Group 34
De Putti, Lya 35
de Trafford, Violet 33, *79*
Dennys, Joyce 37, *165*
Derp, Clotilde von 14, 30, *55*
Deskwork at the British Union of Fascists 148

Deslys, Gaby 31
d'Este, Beatrice 33
D.H. Evans (department store) 32
Diaghilev, Serge 12, 30
Diez-Dührkopp, Minya 33
Dog Cemetery, Hyde Park 21, *156*
Dollfuss, Engelbert 36
Dorien Leigh Galleries 34
Dorien Leigh photographic agency 38
Dorien Leigh picture library 13, 14
'Dorothy Darnit' (comic strip) 23, *23*
Dresden International Exhibition of Photography 28
Drinking tea in the busmen's canteen 139
Duff-Gordon, Lucy, Lady 32
Dührkopp, Rudolf 33
    Emil Hoppé (portrait)*26*
Dutch West Indies 41

E
Edwardes, George 30
Einstein, Albert *106*
Eliot, T.S. 32
Elizabeth, Queen, the Queen Mother (née Bowes-Lyon) 53, *108*, *109*
Ellis, Henry Havelock *104*
Emerson, Peter Henry, *Life and Landscape on the Norfolk Broads* 17
E.O. Hoppé Estate Collection, Pasadena, USA 13, 14, 19
Epstein, Jacob 16, 31, 35, *81*
    bust of Iris Tree 21
Evans, F.H. 28
Evans, Walker 21
Eve 31
Exiting Tottenham Court Road Underground Station 141

F
Fall, Leo, *The Dollar Princess* 30
Felling trees at Rag, Galhampton,164
Feuchtwanger, Lion 35
Fine Art Society 30
Fisherman, The 32
Flag-making for the Coronation at Whiteley's 127
Flora, Flower Lady, Piccadilly Circus 118
Flory, Regine 31
Flower Seller 18, *117*
Fokina, Vera *53*
Fokine, Michel 30, *53*
Fonteyn, Margot *2*, 11, 37, *56*

Fortini, Mario 27
Foxcroft, Frederick *16*, 17
Franco-British Exhibition, White City 36
Frost, Robert 32

G
Galsworthy, John 35
Garrett, Arthur 27
Gauthier, Lucien 24
  Tahitian Beauty 24
George V, King 13, 16, 32, *107*
George VI, King 53, *109*
Gerrard, Teddie 14, *74*
Gibson, Charles Dana 35
Gilman, Harold 35
*Girls at swimming pool, Borstal Institute,
  Aylesbury 160*
*Girls dancing to gramophone, Borstal
  Institute, Aylesbury 161*
Gish, Lillian *69*
Gluck 34, *88*
Gough, Sylvia *75*
Goupil Gallery 19, 30, 35
Graham, Martha *54*
Granville-Barker, Harley 30

H
Haggard, H. Rider 32
Haitian Beauty 42
Hardy, Thomas 16, 32, *93*
Harlem Renaissance 13
Hartley, Marsden *82*
Harvey, Lilian 35
Hawthorne, Eileen 14, *77*
Helm, Brigitte 35, *70*
Heywood, Cecil 27
Highly Respectable 19, *119*
His Majesty's Prisoners of War Fund 33
Hitler, Adolf 38
Hollyer, Frederick 28
Home Workers 18, *117*
Hoppé, Emil (architect) 26
Hoppé, Emil Otto *167*
  Christmas card *27*
  as Dorien Leigh 13–14, 34, 38
  as James Carr 38
  photographs from one-man show at RPS *29*
  portrait by Beaton *169*
  portrait by Dührkoop *26*
  textile design *12*
  Book of Fair Women, The 13, *14*, 15, 18, 19,
    22–4, 32, 33–4, 35
  Camera on Unknown London 37
  'Day in the Museums, A' 36
  Deutsche Arbeit 36
  Glory that Was Grub Street, The 32
  Gods of Modern Grub Street 32
  Hundred Thousand Exposures 11, 12–13
  Image of London, The 36
  London Types 14, 15, 17, 19, 36, 116
  Old Ladies 37
  'Photographing the Maharaja of Udaipur' 36
  Picturesque Great Britain 36
  'Rhythm of Perfect Types' 22
  Romantic America 36
  Self-portrait 8, 11
  'Study in Ethnography, A' 15
  Taken from Life 15, 19, *36*, 116
  'Training the Army Officer' 36
  see also E.O. Hoppé Estate Collection,
    Pasadena, USA
Hoppé, Frank Sidney 31, 36

Hoppé, Marion (née Bliersbach) 26
Hoppé, Muriel Marion 31
Hoppé, Philipp 26
Howe, Graham 14
Hunt, Violet *101*

I
Ibsen, Henrik 30
Ingram, Bruce 29
International Group of Art Photographers 28
International Photographic Exhibition,
  Dresden (1909) 17
*In the waiting room at the dog hospital,
  Croydon 157*

J
James, Henry 30, 32, *98*
Jay, Bill 13
Jerome, Jerome K. 32
Joan (hippo) 37, *154*
John, Augustus 35
Jordan, Mimi *72*
Joyce Dennys, Budleigh Salterton 165

K
Karsavina, Tamara 12, 30, *30*, *49*, *51*, *52*
Kipling, Rudyard 30, 32, *92*
Kollwitz, Käthe *84*
Koo, Madame Wellington 33, *34*
Korff, Kurt 35

L
Lambert, Revd F.C. 26
Lang, Fritz 35, *71*
Lavery, Sir John 31, *33*
Lavery, Lady (Hazel Martyn) 32, *33*, 34, 35, *42*, *79*
Leica I camera 14
Leverhulme, Lord 34
Lewis, (John) Furley 26, 27
Li Ching-Fong 29
Lindsay, Sir Coutts, 31
Linked Ring 28
Llewellyn Davies, Peter *95*
Lloyd George, David *110*
London Salon of Photography 28
London School of Economics, Shaw Papers 19
Loos, Anita *102*
Lorant, Stefan 32
Losch, Tilly 14, *59*
Lucile (fashion house) 32
Ludwig, Prince Regent of Bavaria 28

M
Mackintosh, Charles Rennie 35
Madame Tussaud's 37, *153*
Maeterlinck, Maurice 32
Making waxworks at Madame Tussaud's 153
Mansell Collection 14
Manship, Paul *83*
Maori Chief 113
Marinetti, Filippo Tommaso 30, *78*
Marion Hoppé et Cie 26
Marriott, Charles 34
Mary, Queen 32–3, *32*
Masefield, John 32, *100*
Massereene and Ferrard, Viscountess 33, *42*
Maugham, W. Somerset *96*
Mensdorf-Pouilly, Count Albert von 30
Mestrovic, Ivan 31
Metternich, Count Paul-Wolff 30
Meyer, Baron Adolphe de 32
Millais House (7 Cromwell Place) 12, 19, 21,
  30–1, 34, 35, 38

Millais, Sir John Everett 12, 31
Mills, E.H. 26
Molière, *Le malade imaginaire* 12
Monolulu, Ras Prince *132*
Morton, Cavendish 28
Mrs Bennett 117
Mrs Brandt 168
Munkácsi, Martin 36
Munns, Bernard 32
Mussolini, Benito 14, 35, *111*

N
Nash, Paul 35
National Photographic Record
  Association (NPRA) 17
Natural History Museum 36
Naturalist mounting a stuffed bird 155
Nepal, Prince of 36
New York 118, 119
New York Times 33
Nicholson, William 14, *80*
Nightwatchman, Bank of England 146
Nightwatchman at Ely Place 147
Nijinsky, Vaslav 12, 30, *47*, *50*
Nilsson, Anna Q. 33

O
Ochs, Siegfried 35
O'Dell, Catherine Stackpool *152*
Odle, Alan *89*
Oedipus Rex 30
O'Neill, Eugene 32
Orbis Terrarum series 36
Organist at Old Mill Church, Reigate 162
Organ of the Royal Albert Hall, The 159

P
Palerme, Gina 11, 31, *66*, *67*
Park, Bertram 28
Parlo, Dita 35, *36*
Parr, Martin 21–2
Passengers on a bus, 138
Pavlova, Anna 12
*Pearlies, Master WilliamDennis
  Simmons, The 131*
*Percussion band, Roedean school,
  Brighton, 162*
Phillpotts, Eden 35
Philpot, Glyn 35
photojournalism 36–8
*Phrenologist Catherine Stackpool
  O'Dell, London 152*
*Physical Education, The King's
  School, Canterbury 125*
Pictorialism 14
Pinero, Arthur Wing 30
Plough, The 35
*Policeman at Serpentine Lido,
  Hyde Park 123*
Ponting, H.G. (Herbert) 26, 27
Porter, Marie von der 26
Postman 119
Pound, Ezra *91*
Prime of Life 117
Princess White Deer 43
Puvis de Chavannes, Pierre 21

R
Ray-Jones, Tony 21
  Glyndebourne 22
*Refreshment Rooms, West India
  Dock Road 135*

Regent Street 143
Reinhardt, Max 12, 13, *60*
    Miracle, The 30
    Sumurun 30
Ribbentrop, Joachim von 38
Ridge, William Pett 19
Riefenstahl, Leni 35
Rimsky-Korsakov, Nikolai,
    Scheherazade 30
Robeson, Paul *61*
Roedean school 37, *162*
    singing in chapel *37*
Roerich, Nicholas *85*
Ross Verlag 35
Rosse, Herman 34
Rouilly, Guy 37–8
Royal Albert Hall, organ 21, *159*
Royal Photographic Society 26, 27,
    28, 29
Rumanian Gipsy 168

S
Sackville-West, Vita *97*
Sadler's Wells Ballet 37
St Denis, Ruth 30
Salle, Marguerite *105*
Sander, August 17
    Face of our Time, The 17
    *Mother and Daughter: Farmer's
        Wife and Miner's Wife* 17, *17*
    People of the Twentieth Century 17
Sandhurst Royal Military College, 124
*Sandwich man advertising Shafi Hindustan
    Restaurant, Gerrard Street 134*
Sant, James 30
Savoy Hotel waiters feeding birds, 142
Scarborough Post 23
Second World War 13
Sergeant, Elizabeth 32
Shadowland 32
Shakespeare, William, *Romeo and Juliet* 31
Shaw, George Bernard 13, 17, 18, 19–21, *20,*
    27, 30, 32, *114, 115*
    cloud study 20, *21*
    Pygmalion 20–1
Shawn, Ted 14, 30, *44, 54*
Sheringham, George 35
Sinhalese Gentleman, A 119
Sketching, Hyde Park, 123
Sleeping on the street, Trafalgar Square, 149
snack bar counter, 21, *136–7*
Snowden, Philip 28
Speakers' Corner, Hyde Park 122
Spessivtseva, Olga *46*
Sphere, The 28
Steichen, Edward 28
Stieglitz, Alfred 28
Stone, Sir Benjamin 17, 28
    Farm Labourers 16
    Frederick Foxcroft 16
Strand, Paul 21
Strang, William 14, 29, *87*
Straus, Oscar, *The Chocolate Soldier* 30
Street musicians 126
street pictures 15, 16
*Student ironing in the pantry,
    Lady Margaret Hall 163*
Studies from the Russian Ballet 30
studio photography 14
Swinburne Ballet 33

T
*Tableau of Lute-Playing and
    Singing Angels 166*

Tagore, Rabindranath *90*
Tennant, Stephen 34
    The Boy who Saw the Fairies 34
Terry, Ellen 31, *63*
Thomas, Edward 32, *103*
*Thomas Williams, Superintendent of
    Buckingham Palace 145*
Thomson, John, *Street Life in London* 17
Tillers of the Soil 30
Tokugawa, Mrs 33
Tree, Sir Hubert Beerbohm 28, 29
Tree, Iris 21
Tweedie, Mrs Alec 28, *28*
typology 16–19, 22

U
Ufa Film Studios 35
undercover photography 21

V
Vanity Fair 32
Vaughan Williams, Ralph 32
Vedic scholar, Gwalior 118
Vedrenne, J.E. 30
Versailles, Treaty of 10
Vesselier, Constance (Hebe) 32, 34, *41*
Victoria and Albert Museum 30–1
Vienna Secession 27
Visitor, The 27
Vogue 32
Vorticism 13

W
Waitress, Miss Vyse, the original 'Nippy', 144
Walter, Bruno 35
Warburg, J.C. 26
Ward, H. Snowden 26, 27
Weber, Carl Maria von 30
Weber, Max 34
Westminster Underground Station, 140
West, Rebecca *99*
What Next 27
White Horse Eagle, Big Chief *112*
Whiteley's (department store) 38, *129*
Wilde, Oscar 16
Willoughby, Biddy 14, *76*
women's suffrage movement 24
Wong, Anna May *73*
Woods, Al 35
Wu Kang 21

Y
Young Brahmin Woman, Guntakal 118

Z
*Zookeeper, Ernie Bowman and
    Hippopotamus, Joan 154*